Prayers
for
Freedom
over Worry
and Anxiety

Bruce Wilkinson

HARVEST HOUSE PUBLISHERS
EUGENE, OREGON

Cover by Rightly Designed

PRAYERS FOR FREEDOM OVER WORRY AND ANXIETY

Copyright © 2017 Bruce Wilkinson
Published by Harvest House Publishers
Eugene, Oregon 97402
www.harvesthousepublishers.com

ISBN 978-0-7369-7179-9 (pbk.)
ISBN 978-0-7369-7180-5 (eBook)

Library of Congress Cataloging-in-Publication Data

Names: Wilkinson, Bruce, author.
Title: Prayers for freedom over worry and anxiety / Bruce Wilkinson
Description: Eugene, Oregon : Harvest House Publishers, 2017. |
Identifiers: LCCN 2017014018 (print) | LCCN 2017022898 (ebook) | ISBN 9780736971805 (ebook) | ISBN 9780736971799 (pbk.)
Subjects: LCSH: Worry—Religious aspects—Christianity. | Anxiety—Religious aspects—Christianity. | Peace of mind—Religious aspects—Christianity. | Prayers. | Prayer—Christianity.
Classification: LCC BV4908.5 (ebook) | LCC BV4908.5 .W555 2017 (print) | DDC 242/.4—dc23
LC record available at https://lccn.loc.gov/2017014018

Printed in the United States of America

21 22 23 24 25 / BP-SK / 10 9 8 7 6 5 4

Dedicated to all who long to leave worry behind and walk in ongoing peace and contentment.

May you find practical biblical answers and meaningful prayers within these pages.

May your prayer with us each day be exactly what you needed for that day!

Acknowledgments

This book could only be possible with the creative and writing skills of my talented editor, who requested anonymity.

Thank you for your heart for the Lord and sensitivity to others, as demonstrated throughout this book.

Contents

Introduction

If you are like the rest of us, you struggle with anxiety and worry from time to time. Don't you? Since you do, how would you like proven Anxiety Answers that work every single time? I'm not overpromising or overstating the truth even a little.

Before we reveal those effective solutions to anxiety, however, how about a little self-examination? Pause for a moment, and let's do a little self-diagnosis by answering the questions below as honestly as possible.

1. You experience feelings of worry or anxiety this often:

    ☐ Numerous times in a day

    ☐ Maybe once a day or so

    ☐ A couple of times a week

    ☐ Once a week

    ☐ Hardly ever

    ☐ Never

If you checked "Never," then see if you can return this book and get your money back. Or give it away to someone you know who has challenges with anxiety!

2. On a scale of 1 (very low) to 10 (very high), how strong and bothersome are your feelings of anxiety and worry? _____

3. Have you ever taken medicine or drugs to help you cope with anxiety? _____

4. When you feel anxious, how do you normally cope? Circle or check off the tactics that you usually use to relieve your anxiety:

   ☐ At times, I use drugs to cope.

   ☐ At times, I use alcohol to cope.

   ☐ At times, I use pornography to cope.

   ☐ At times, I overeat to cope.

   ☐ At times, I slide into depression and sleep far too much to cope.

   ☐ At times, I exercise to cope.

   ☐ At times, I isolate myself from everyone else to cope.

   ☐ At times, I overwork to cope.

   ☐ At times, I watch TV and/or surf the Web to cope.

   ☐ At times, I pray and read my Bible to cope.

5. How hard do you anticipate it will be for you to rid yourself of anxiety and worry?

   ☐ I don't believe I can ever conquer my anxiety.

☐ I believe I will have to stay on anxiety drugs to be free enough.

☐ I believe it will take me years to conquer my anxiety.

☐ I believe it will take far too much effort and won't work.

☐ I believe if the solutions really work, I can be free of anxiety right now.

I'll never forget a three-minute conversation I had with a young man at a men's conference who lamented to me privately that he was totally unable to stop using pornography. I smiled and said, "Well, it appears that you have convinced yourself that there isn't any solution, and under no circumstance could you stop using pornography instantly. Am I right?" He nodded in agreement. I continued, "It's because your sex drive is so much stronger than most men's, right?" He nodded even more, sensing I understood his dilemma.

"So, if you were looking at pornography in your bedroom in the middle of the night and your mother unexpectedly walked in, what would you do?" He nearly shouted, "Man, I would shut down my computer instantly!" Then I nodded and nodded. He got it. Do you get it?

It's of great value to hold one simple Bible verse in your mind. In fact, you probably already know it: "Be anxious for nothing" (Philippians 4:6 NKJV). The words "be anxious" are translated from the Greek word *merimnao*. We'll come back to that word later, but right now focus on three important facts about that verb.

First, "be anxious" is in the present tense—not past tense or future tense. Why? No one can be anxious yesterday when it is today. And, it's just as impossible to be anxious in the future today. Anxiety only can occur in the present.

Second, "be anxious" is in the active voice, not the passive voice. That means that not "being anxious" is something you actively do yourself. Someone else cannot "be anxious" for you. Why not? Because 100 percent of anxiety dwells only within you. Even more striking is the fact that this verb is active, not passive. You are the only one whose action can lead to anxiousness, meaning no one—and nothing—can make you anxious. Not your spouse, your child, your parents, your boss, your government. Nope.

That's why two people can experience the exact same crisis and one becomes anxious and the other doesn't. One person responded by choosing anxiety, and the other person chose not to be anxious.

You and you alone are 100 percent in control of your anxiety. You are the only person who can activate anxiety within you. So with that in mind, it's time to break free from the *big lie* that something or someone made you anxious.

Are you ready for the third fact about that verb "be anxious"? This final characteristic of the verb is the most important: It's an imperative. God reveals a direct command to all of us: Don't choose anxiety under any circumstances. If you do, you have chosen to sin. You have willfully chosen to activate your anxiety in direct disobedience to God's will in your life.

As you know, God never commands us to do something unless we can obey Him. So, in contrast to the *big lie*, here's the *big truth*: You have always been in total and complete control of your anxiety. At all times, and under every circumstance, you can always choose not to activate your anxiety. God granted that freedom to all of us. Please note: The only exception to this is if your anxiety is drug-related or chemical-related.

So, if you checked any of the other choices under question #5 except the last one—"I can be free of anxiety right now"—you have been deluded into believing the lie. Remember that young man with the pornography problem? He was addicted until his mother walked in—then all of a sudden, he discovered massive already-existing reserves of self-control! He was able to stop instantly. As I continued my conversation with the young man, I smiled and said, "Maybe you should ask your mother to follow you around all day and night!"

Before going to the next section, take a big breath and say out loud, "I am always entirely free to choose not to respond to whatever life throws at me. I reject the lie that it's 'Just the way I am' or that 'I cannot help myself.' Even if my life is in the pits, I have control over anxiety and worry."

Let's analyze anxiety for a few moments further. First of all, why do we say "I feel anxious" instead of "I think anxious"? It's because all of us experience the *feelings* of anxiety. Therefore, too many of us assume that we cannot control our feelings, that we are helpless against the onslaught of anxious emotions. But once again, we are mistaken, since God instructs us to control our emotions. For example, consider these two commands: "Love one another fervently with a pure heart" (1 Peter 1:22 NKJV) and "Do not fear" (Luke 12:7).

One thing should be obvious at this point: All of us are much more in control of our anxiety than we may have ever imagined!

So what, then, is God's answer to our anxieties and worries? Let's take a look at each part of Philippians 4:6: "Be anxious for nothing, but in everything…" (NKJV). The contrast between *nothing* and *everything* is clear: God leaves absolutely no room for any person to have any anxiety of any kind at any time. We are to be anxious *for nothing*. At this point, if you are going to live a truly anxiety-free life, here's an important point to notice: The rest of Philippians 4:6-8 actually reveals the supernatural answer to all anxiety. God's answer, in plain language. You won't have to look anywhere else beyond this short Bible passage to find the answer.

In only three verses, God lays out three steps that, if followed, will work for you—100 percent of the time! In fact, if you are anxious right now, use them and experience a stunning victory in only a few moments.

> *Step #1:* What to do when you are anxious (your part)

> *Step #2:* What God will do with your anxiety if you do your part (His part)

> *Step #3:* What to do to become "anxiety-resistant" in the future (your future option)

Let's examine these three steps in this short passage so you will be able to find quick relief for all anxiety.

Step #1: What to Do When You Are Anxious

> *Be anxious for nothing, but in everything by prayer and supplication with thanksgiving let your requests be made known to God* (Philippians 4:6 NKJV).

Anytime you start to feel anxiety, remember these words: "Let your requests be made known to God." The first step is to pray—that's the reason why my editor and I have written this book, *Prayers for Freedom over Worry and Anxiety*, for you.

I'm sure you have tried praying about your most difficult anxieties in the past—and I would anticipate that your response might be, "Yes, I tried prayer, and it didn't work." Would you like to know why it didn't work? The reason is, you must follow the specific instructions in this verse and not skip any step—then you will discover the amazing experience of victory every single time.

It's like making a cake and forgetting one critical ingredient. The result is a cake that flops! Yes, you made the cake, but one or more of the necessary ingredients was missing. No matter how carefully you made the cake, no matter how sincerely you wanted it to turn out right, and no matter for whom you were baking the cake, the cake flopped.

This verse contains three specific ingredients for enjoying God's amazing answer to your worry and anxiety.

First, you must pray to God about your situation.

Second, you must not only pray; you must supplicate. *Supplication* is a translation of the Greek noun *deesis*, which is different from just praying. It means "to ask or entreat God because of a specific need." The specific need is the very situation or person that is triggering your feelings of anxiety. To supplicate means asking God to intervene in the face of your situation.

Third, and perhaps most important of all, you must thank God for the very thing that is surfacing your anxiety. This step is counter to what we want to do, isn't it? Why would we thank God for the very thing that is the source of our turbulent, negative emotions? What a powerful secret! The moment you thank God for this opportunity, you exercise your trust in Him and obey His command not to sin with anxiety. By flipping it over and thanking God for that difficulty, you demonstrate your faith in His power.

Anxiety cannot exist in the presence of gratitude!

By presenting God your requests with thanksgiving, you are practicing 1 Thessalonians 5:16-18: "Rejoice always, pray without ceasing, in everything give thanks; for this is the will of God in Christ Jesus for you" (NKJV). Once again, the words are in the present active imperative. This is only tested when something occurs in life that we strongly dislike, and it's hard to find any reason to "give thanks." Since this is a command, you and I both realize that we can choose to obey, but it's not always very easy.

This just happened to me in the last 40 minutes. As is often true, the Lord seems to enjoy putting me through numerous tests on the very truth for which I'm either teaching or writing a book. He wants my communication to be a bit more real and visceral because I had to struggle through the very issue over which I'm trying to help someone else to experience victory.

Here's what happened. On Tuesday, I lost my small Day-Timer calendar for the entire year. It recorded scores of important meetings that I had forgotten to make a copy of in case I did misplace it. I panicked, knowing I couldn't remember even half of all the events, meetings, deadlines, and speaking engagements. So I did what anyone would do—I emptied my computer case and briefcase; looked through the drawers of my desk; checked my dresser, my jackets, my shirt pockets, and my car and trunk; called the office in case I had left it there; looked in all the drawers in the kitchen and through all my course materials; etc.

My anxiety increased every day. Then my loving wife Darlene checked everywhere as I repeated all of these steps a second and third time. I prayed, but no help. Darlene prayed, but no help. My sister Pat prayed, but no help. The next day, my anxiety had doubled again. I looked again, prayed again, and felt irritated that God did not help me the way He had in the past.

Today is Saturday, and I had to make a couple of telephone calls just to make sure I wouldn't miss some important meetings with my team next week at the Teach Every Nation offices in Atlanta, Georgia. At lunch today, my anxieties had nearly reached the panic level about missing a meeting or conference call. But as I walked out of the kitchen on the way to my home office to finish this chapter so I could meet the Monday deadline, I took stock of my situation and realized I was filled with anxiety.

As I walked down the three stairs into the garage, I thought, *Practice the answer for all anxiety*. It occurred to me that I'm not thankful in the least for this crisis, and I also felt a bit irritated that heaven would not at least give me a hint about the location of my lost Day-Timer. When my foot hit the garage floor, I started forcing myself to thank the Lord. I thanked Him for the frustration, for my lost calendar, for not knowing what to do, for the potential of disappointing others by missing meetings, and more. I thanked Him all the way through the garage to my office door. By the time I opened that door, my anxiety had disappeared! And, I forgot about my missing calendar.

I sat down on my chair, opened my computer, and started cleaning some dishes off the corner of the desk. Right there—I couldn't believe it—the calendar was under a plate. Now, I know I had looked on my desk at least five times. If you had been there, you would have heard me laughing and laughing! I told God, "I get it! This little anxiety test—which I had failed for 4.5 days in a row—was a reality check." After praying and thanking God for the very issues that I felt anxious about, and after naming them one by one, I experienced the next part of the verse. I was sure that heaven was exploding in laughter with me at God's lesson plan for this chapter!

Step #2: What God Will Do with Your Anxiety If You Do Your Part

When you pray and make your requests known to God with thanksgiving regarding your anxiety and its causes, then something quite remarkable occurs in response: God promises you a supernatural response. God hears these kinds of prayers and promises to always answer them. Unlike many of our

prayers—to which God may respond with a *no* or a *not yet*—
God always answers *yes* to this particular prayer. Read Philippians 4:6-7 to see His clear and direct promise for you:

> *Be anxious for nothing, but in everything by prayer*
> *and supplication, with thanksgiving, let your requests*
> *be made known to God; and the peace of God, which*
> *surpasses all understanding, will guard your hearts*
> *and your minds through Christ Jesus* (NKJV).

When you are filled with anxiety and pray with thanksgiving
about that very discomforting circumstance, then God supernaturally intervenes in your life and gives you a priceless gift:
"the peace of God." God doesn't increase *your* peace; instead, He
gives you *His* peace. His peace overwhelms all your anxiety and
literally destroys it by replacing it with His supernatural peace.

But you must recognize one shocking fact: Even after God
grants you His peace, the underlying cause of your anxiety and
worry hasn't changed! What *did* change was your mental and
emotional response to that situation. The causes of your anxiety are still present. Since nothing external changed, how can
you experience God's gift of His peace? The answer lies in the
power of God's peace—His peace is so strong that it "surpasses
all understanding." How exactly does that work?

The word "surpasses" is translated from the Greek word
hyperecho, which literally means "to hold above, to be above, to
be superior to." God's peace enters your life because you met
God's universal requirement—prayer, supplication, and gratitude—and He responds by surpassing your anxious thoughts
and feelings with His sovereign peace. His peace is so far above
and superior in its positive power that it drowns all your negative fears and worries. God wipes them clean; He erases the
words *your anxieties* off the blackboard of your soul and writes

MY PEACE in big, all-capital letters, leaving no trace of your worry.

I described the replacement of your anxiety with His peace as "supernatural" because God's peace *simply isn't natural*. It's above—"super"—natural. You cannot explain why you now are filled with peace because God's peace surpasses all your understanding. The peace you feel isn't your peace or any other person's peace, but rather God's supernatural peace. You called out for God's help, and God responded with His gift.

How do you know this will happen to you? The word for "surpassing" is the participle *hyperecho*, and it is in the present active form—which means that when you pray/supplicate/thank God, then at that very moment (in the present) God acts on your behalf. You don't generate your own peace; God actively gifts His peace to you right then, in your present difficult moment. How gracious of our God!

Remember my anxiety over my lost calendar? As soon as I prayed, asked God for help with my anxious thoughts, and thanked Him for my terrible situation, guess what happened? God immediately poured out His peace into my emotions and thoughts. How long did that take? The amount of time it took to walk from one side of the garage to the other. A mere few seconds. I didn't ask Him for peace, but I did thank Him for the situation.

You don't need to ask God for His peace, but if you meet His requirements, He will always respond by keeping His end of the arrangement. But recognize the surprising fact that my calendar was still lost! His peace is granted even when the problem persists. My emotions were supernaturally transformed in mere seconds. Underscore in your mind this truth: Anxiety is your response to a situation, and not the situation itself.

As a person who has practiced this passage many times over

the decades, I give you my affirmation: This truth has always worked in my life. Why? Because God keeps His word for anyone who meets His requirements!

You might think that God's peace would be His "final answer" for our anxiety and worry, but amazingly, He goes beyond what we could imagine. Read the rest of verse 7: "and the peace of God, which surpasses all understanding, will guard your hearts and minds through Christ Jesus." Even as I write this to you, I'm once again stunned by the gracious kindness of God. His peace is not only granted instantly, but also His peace positions itself to guard you from new anxiety attacks on the same issue. The peace of God stands as a powerful protector in this area of your life. In fact, God's stated promise is that His peace will "guard your hearts and minds through Christ Jesus."

The words "will guard" are translated from a very specific Greek word *phroureo*, which is a military term meaning "to keep by guarding, to keep under guard." This verb is used to describe a garrison of soldiers who provide protection against any and all enemies. This same word is used twice in 2 Corinthians 11:32: "In Damascus the governor, under Aretas the king, was guarding the city of the Damascenes *with a garrison,* desiring to arrest me" (NKJV).

Once God pours His peace into you, you'd better be on guard for anxious thoughts and feelings lest they return, right? Nope. I don't know if you are ready for the rest of God's remarkable revelation, but the verb *phroureo* is in the future active indicative form—not the present tense. In other words, God not only gifts peace to you at that moment (present tense of surpassing), but He continues to actively take responsibility for guarding that gift of peace. Nothing can destroy or weaken it in the future. God gives His peace in the present, then guards your heart and thoughts into the future.

This passage reveals the twofold response of God to our anxieties. First, God pours out a surpassing peace into our lives in the present; and second, God stands guard to ensure His peace remains in your life in this area.

Please remember this seminal fact: The cause of your anxieties hasn't changed. What has changed is your response to that situation. You chose to delegate your anxieties to the Lord and affirm your thankfulness for whatever God is doing in your life through that difficulty. Since the underlying cause of your anxieties hasn't changed, won't your anxious thoughts soon flood back? Read again about the two specific areas where God's peace will stand guard for you: "[He] will guard your hearts and minds through Christ Jesus." God will protect you in the future from both thoughts and feelings about this specific area. Once again, God does more than we could think or imagine!

Step #3: What to Do to Become "Anxiety-Resistant" in the Future

For those who desire to become "anxiety-resistant" in the future, the next verse lays out how to achieve that wonderful state of ongoing peace in all areas of your life. In normal situations, all our anxieties are rooted in our thoughts, which then give birth to our anxious feelings. Unless your physical body in some way is off-balance, anxious feelings can only develop from anxious or fearful thoughts. Therefore, the key to a life free of anxiety is to take your thoughts captive, not permitting any thoughts that would be outside of God's will for you. Look at the characteristics of anxiety-free thoughts, as seen in the next verse, Philippians 4:8:

> *Finally, brethren, whatever things are true, whatever things are noble, whatever things are just, whatever things are pure, whatever things are lovely, whatever things are*

of good report, if there is any virtue and if there is anything praiseworthy—meditate on these things (NKJV).

The verb "meditate" is a future imperative—meaning that since you now have peace in the present, make sure to guard against falling into another mindset that generates anxiety for you. How? By focusing your thoughts on the true, noble, just, pure, lovely, good, virtuous, and praiseworthy. When you obey God's command to think/meditate on the positive rather than on the negative, guess what will be impossible? An anxious thought! If you have no anxious thoughts, then you will have no anxious feelings! But, if worrisome and anxious thoughts and feelings do creep in for whatever reason, you now know exactly what to do!

With that in mind, you can understand why my editor and I structured this book, *Prayers for Freedom over Worry and Anxiety*, the way we did. Along with our publisher, we researched and selected the key topics that people are anxious and worried about, and treated each one with the same fourfold structure:

1. Preparing Our Hearts for Prayer
2. Pursuing God's Presence in Prayer
3. Practice of Prayer
4. Personal Prayer Thoughts, Answers, and Reminders

We hope and pray that this little gem of a book will be a great help to you personally. May your life not only experience the blessings that God promised when you fulfill His prerequisites, but even more than that, we pray you will become so "anxiety-resistant" that you will rarely experience an anxious feeling in the years ahead.

With prayers for God's surpassing peace,
Bruce Wilkinson
President, Teach Every Nation

1

Unknown Health Issues

Preparing Our Hearts for Prayer

Unknown health issues can often plague our hearts and our minds more than the known ones. The what-ifs provide no boundaries or limitations, leaving our thoughts to wander deeply and freely in worry. Before we know it, we've diagnosed ourselves with a serious disease and are planning for the worst. We don't want to succumb to this what-if anxiety every time we experience a very normal ache, pain, or abnormality. Have you ever asked yourself:

> Is the lump cancerous or simply a swollen lymph node?
>
> Is the pain in my chest heart disease, a heart attack, or one too many pieces of pizza?
>
> Is my kidney inflamed, or is my appendix about to burst?
>
> Wait, where is the appendix anyhow? And *where are* my kidneys?

In today's world, with such easy access to all sorts of media, information, medical websites, forums, and even our friends' and family's health statuses, we have no lack of possible outcomes for any discomfort we may feel. They say that ignorance is bliss, and when it comes to unknown health issues, that may very well be the case. With the rise of health and illness information at our fingertips, too much knowledge may be contributing to our worry or even worsening our stress. That is not to say you shouldn't follow up with a trained medical professional if symptoms persist, but you should also be mindful that "for as he thinks within himself, so he is" (Proverbs 23:7).

Did you know that worrying about your health can actually worsen your health? Identified impacts of worry and anxiety on the body include: stomach pain, acne, weight gain (slower metabolism), body aches, hair loss, loss of libido, heartburn, and more. This is because when you worry, your body releases hormones called cortisone and adrenaline that are provided by God to equip you for real danger. The only problem with worry is that your body cannot tell the difference between real or perceived danger.

Because worry arouses a feeling of impending doom, your body responds by elevating your hormone levels—even though the "danger" is something you only imagined! When these stress hormones are free to roam in your bloodstream over a prolonged period of time, they can become toxic to your glands, heart, digestion, and nervous system. This can eventually lead to real health issues and real damage to any number of systems and organs in your body. Our bodies simply weren't designed to remain in a constant state of alert, otherwise known as "fight or flight" panic, any longer than what's necessary to trigger an appropriate response to danger.

So what's the antidote to worrying about unknown health issues that seem to lurk around every corner? We can overcome consistent worry and anxiety by intentionally seeking a mindset of peace through prayer. Yes, you should follow up on any ongoing physical symptoms with a trained professional; but in the meantime when there are no diagnosed ailments, try to live in peace rather than a heightened fear of what may happen in the future. Rather than having the cells in your body washed over by a constant flow of cortisol, wash them with the Word of God, which will bring life to your bones and joy to your heart. If you are not a fan of reading Scripture (or even reading at all), there are free audio versions of the Bible available through a variety of useful apps in the app store. Listening to, meditating on, and ingesting the truth of God's Word is one way of replacing thoughts of worry with thoughts of victory and life.

Pursuing God's Presence in Prayer

> Beloved, I pray that in all respects you may prosper and be in good health, just as your soul prospers (3 John 1:2).

> A joyful heart is good medicine, but a broken spirit dries up the bones (Proverbs 17:22).

> Blessed is the man who trusts in the LORD and whose trust is the LORD. For he will be like a tree planted by the water, that extends its roots by a stream and will not fear when the heat comes; but its leaves will be green, and it will not be anxious in a year of drought nor cease to yield fruit (Jeremiah 17:7-8).

Practice of Prayer

Gracious heavenly Father, Your Word tells me that I am blessed when I put my trust in You. This trust keeps me from fear and worry when difficulties come. Your Word also says I will not be anxious in a year of drought. Trust is a powerful weapon against worry and anxiety. Strengthen my trust in You, Lord. Increase my capacity to trust. Remind me of Your presence in such a way that joy fills my heart.

About this particular pain, symptom, or health concern—I ask that You will do one of three things. One, please remove the symptoms (aches, pain, lump, etc.) entirely and quickly. Two, please give me insight into what it truly is. If it is minor, help me treat it myself using a healthy diet, hot packs, or over-the-counter medicine. Or three, Lord, give me the courage to seek professional medical help to diagnose my symptoms quickly. Please lead me to the best doctors, and give them Your wisdom on what is wrong. Please help them to treat me, so that I may be cured quickly. Thank You, God, for answering my prayers. In Christ's name, amen.

Personal Prayer Thoughts, Answers, and Reminders

_____

_____

_____

_____

_____

_____

_____

_____

_____

_____

_____

_____

_____

_____

_____

_____

_____

_____

_____

_____

_____

2

Finances

Preparing Our Hearts for Prayer

Fears about finances often weigh heavy in the background of our emotions. We don't always think about money, but the issue can feel like a low-hanging cloud, darkening our days. This is because so much of what we do—so many of our choices—is dictated by our financial capacity.

> Will we be able to afford a decent college education for our children?
>
> Will we even be able to complete our own education that we desire?
>
> Can we take that vacation we so desperately need?
>
> Can we afford to eat healthy food, rather than the inexpensive processed food so easily at our disposal?
>
> What about rent?
>
> The car note?
>
> Insurance?
>
> Medical bills?
>
> Clothing?
>
> The kids' shoes?

The list could go on ad infinitum. Money really does play a large role in each and every decision we make, so it's understandable that such an important area of life could give rise to worry and anxiety. But did you know that the antidote found in God's Word actually has to do with thinking less highly of money? Over and over we are told to put money in its rightful place. After all, "you cannot serve God and wealth" (Matthew 6:24); and "where your treasure is, there your heart will be also" (Matthew 6:21).

God wants us to understand that if we fix our hope on the uncertainty of money, we will continually be in a state of *emotional* uncertainty. It is God Himself who richly supplies us with all the things that we enjoy. Rather than fixating on whether or not we will have enough for this, that, or the other, we are instructed to use our time, talents, and treasures to benefit those around us. We are to share what we have generously and liberally. And we are to grab hold of the wisdom that tells us we are more than what money could ever buy. What matters most, at the end of the day, never comes from money—things like love, relationships, value, purpose, service, and the Lord. Yes, money matters, and we all have monthly bills to pay, but you will discover a refreshing freedom when you loosen the reins around your finances and begin to use them to help others at a greater level than ever before.

Remember: "One who is gracious to a poor man lends to the LORD, and He will repay him for his good deed" (Proverbs 19:17). You can never outgive God.

Pursuing God's Presence in Prayer

> Do not store up for yourselves treasures on earth, where moth and rust destroy, and where thieves break in and steal. But store up for yourselves treasures in heaven, where neither moth nor rust destroys, and where thieves do not break in or steal;

for where your treasure is, there your heart will be also (Matthew 6:19-21).

Instruct those who are rich in this present world not to be conceited or to fix their hope on the uncertainty of riches, but on God, who richly supplies us with all things to enjoy. Instruct them to do good, to be rich in good works, to be generous and ready to share, storing up for themselves the treasure of a good foundation for the future, so that they may take hold of that which is life indeed (1 Timothy 6:17-19).

He said to them, "Beware, and be on your guard against every form of greed; for not even when one has an abundance does his life consist of his possessions" (Luke 12:15).

Practice of Prayer

Make me a vessel of Your blessing, Lord, so that what You give to me flows through me to others. I know that as I worry about bills to pay and things I long to do, I am moving my eyes off of You and onto the idol of money. Forgive me for putting a commodity ahead of the Creator. Help me to honor You with the firstfruits of all You give to me. Show me how generous You are in return. And give me Your perspective on money so that I will not be entangled in the snare of riches or give the devil an opportunity to cause me to sin.

I release my worry and cares concerning my finances. I hand them all over to You, asking that You will take them far from me. Replace them with a peace that passes understanding and a generous spirit toward those in need. Give me the joy that comes from truly helping others, and teach me to do Your will, O God, because it is in my obedience to You that I will be set free. In Christ's name, amen.

Personal Prayer Thoughts, Answers, and Reminders

_____

_____

_____

_____

_____

_____

_____

_____

_____

_____

_____

_____

_____

_____

_____

_____

_____

_____

_____

3

Mental and Emotional Health

Preparing Our Hearts for Prayer

If you struggle with anxiety or worry, you are not alone. Best estimates say that over 40 million Americans suffer from chronic anxiety, and those are just the ones who have asked for help or are willing to admit it. Many more suffer in silence. Being anxious about what food we eat, how our health is, whether or not we'll get to keep our job, if our marriage is going to survive, driving, flying, public places—you name it—can lead to another form of anxiety. And that is being anxious about anxiety itself.

As anxious thoughts race through your head, hindering you from sleeping or enjoying peace during the day, guard against allowing them to spread into other areas of your life. Don't dwell on anxious questions like: Will my emotions ever be stable? Do I have a chemical imbalance? How do I get rid of this mental fog? Why can't I just be happy? Such questions plague the worrying soul. When you don't guard your thoughts and emotions, anxiety can become a terrible beast of our own making.

There are some practical steps you can take if you are concerned about your mental and emotional health. Since anxious and worrisome thoughts often lead to physical depletion and loss of energy, you may not "feel" like doing any of these. But if you will gradually add one or more to your daily routine, in time you can experience their benefits.

Meditation. Replacing anxious thoughts with sound thoughts of peace, harmony, hope, truth, God's Word, love, and positivity goes a long way toward reducing feelings of worry. Try to spend at least 15 minutes a day clearing your mind of clutter and focusing on Scripture or other positive thoughts. Meditating on the love of God each day has demonstrated significant health benefits. In particular, MRI scans of the brain reveal that the practice of meditation reduces the connection of neural pathways in the medial prefrontal cortex.[1] By loosening these connections, the brain's ability to send signals of fear through these channels is diminished. Because of this, anxiety decreases as well.

Exercise. Working out may be the absolute last thing you want to do when you are feeling worried or anxious, but the act of exercise will reduce your anxiety and have a calming effect on your body. Not only is exercise good for your overall health; when you physically exert yourself, you are releasing neurotransmitters and endorphins that will provide your brain with the capacity to overcome worrisome thoughts. Even if you're simply walking, any amount of exercise opens up the brain's creativity and thought processes in a way that serves to alleviate your stress and anxiety.

Caring for others. God knew exactly what He was saying when He told us that it is better to give than to receive. The very act of thinking of someone else's needs above our own, or bringing happiness and delight to another human being, has been shown to increase our own levels of happiness as well. Somehow the simple act of taking our minds off of ourselves and putting them on someone else helps free us from that which holds us hostage. Make it a habit of helping someone else. Visit the homebound regularly. Go to a nursing home and spend time with someone who receives few or no visitors. Offer to help a neighbor or coworker. Pray for others. Mentor a child or teen. The list of ways to shift your thinking from yourself to someone else in need is endless.

Try these three practical ways to reduce your worry and anxiety about your own mental health. In addition, pray according to God's Word—in faith, knowing that He who began a good work in You will be faithful to complete it. He holds the sun, moon, and earth in place. He can hold you together as well.

Pursuing God's Presence in Prayer

> God has not given us a spirit of timidity, but of power and love and discipline (2 Timothy 1:7).

> We are destroying speculations and every lofty thing raised up against the knowledge of God, and we are taking every thought captive to the obedience of Christ (2 Corinthians 10:5).

> The mind set on the flesh is death, but the mind set on the Spirit is life and peace (Romans 8:6).

Practice of Prayer

Loving God, You have not given me a spirit of timidity. You have not given me a spirit of anxiety. You have not placed these worries in my head and in my heart. In fact, You have given me a spirit of power, and love, and a sound mind. When worries plague me and cause me to question my mental health, I will resist them and renew my mind based upon Your promises. I will not allow myself to stop trusting in You!

You are gracious and come to the aid of those with a humble and dependent heart. You are my strong tower and an ever-present help in times of trouble. I rest knowing that the Christ who could calm the waves and the storm with His words can also calm my heart and mind. Your name Jehovah Shalom signifies a God of peace. Today, I embrace Your shalom into my body, cells, thoughts, emotions, hormones, and soul. Cover me with shalom, Lord.

My mind is kept in perfect peace when I keep my mind focused on You. Remove me from distractions that take my thoughts in the wrong direction. Give me strength to resist the temptation to fill my head with negative thoughts. Help me to resist the fear and danger spoken to me through television, the news, and conversation. Bless me, Lord, with the fruit of a secure heart and a stable mind. Bless me with Your love everlasting, and let it flow gently through my emotions, bringing me calm. I trust in You, God, and You alone, for You are worthy of my faith. In Christ's name, amen.

Personal Prayer Thoughts, Answers, and Reminders

_____

_____

_____

_____

_____

_____

_____

_____

_____

_____

_____

_____

_____

_____

_____

_____

_____

_____

_____

_____

_____

_____

_____

4

Job Security

Preparing Our Hearts for Prayer

Job security, along with job satisfaction, are two very common concerns for most people. This makes sense, considering the average adult spends 30 percent of their life working. If a person lives to be 75 years old, this person will have spent approximately one-third of life working. That's a lot more than we do most anything else. Thus, having a job you love—or, at least, enjoy—and a job you aren't nervous about losing is a very high and normal need for all of us. That said, worrying about your job security comes very naturally when you fall into the trap of believing that your job is the ultimate source of security.

But one of the most misunderstood concepts in the Bible is that of provision. It is a concept that will help anyone who struggles with worry about work. Since we are finite beings who rely heavily, sometimes entirely, on our five senses—what we can see, taste, feel, smell, and hear—we regularly attribute to man what belongs only to God. Job security is one of these areas where we make this mistake far too often.

Your employer may employ you, but God is your source.

Your employer may pay you, but God is your source. Your boss may tell you what to do, when to do it, and how much you get paid for performing your tasks, but God is your source.

Unfortunately, we too easily forget this and become fixated on the middleman. We worry about our job performance. We become anxious about the amount of work we have or don't have to do. We wonder if the paycheck will keep coming, if the commission will keep calculating, or if someone else could possibly replace us. Those are normal feelings and thoughts. We all feel replaceable at some time or another.

Many of us also worry that the economy will suffer or the industry and business sector we work in will take a hit. We watch the news to see what trade deals the government is making today, or which ones they are denying. We may wonder how that will impact our job and also our income.

Cutbacks. Pink slips. Downsizing. Call it what you will: Thoughts of these can lead to anxiety.

But the antidote to worrying about your job security is remembering Who your source is. Not the government. Not your employer. Not even the economy. God is your source. When you intentionally commit your works to the Lord—whether you're working as a bus driver, an accountant, a debate coach, or anything else—God will establish your plans. God Himself will strengthen you and set you securely in your service to Him at your optimal location. That may be where you work now, or He may want to transition you to someplace even better. Focus not as much on the location of your job but on the One who gives it. Locations and duties may change, but the Provider never does. And if your optimal location is where you work now, always remember that if God has opened this door for you—*no* person can close it or take it away. He has a purpose for you to fulfill. And when you make His purpose your driving passion, you are entirely secure.

Pursuing God's Presence in Prayer

> Commit your works to the LORD and your plans will be established (Proverbs 16:3).

> I thank Christ Jesus our Lord, who has strengthened me, because He considered me faithful, putting me into service (1 Timothy 1:12).

> If you have run with footmen and they have tired you out, then how can you compete with horses? If you fall down in a land of peace, how will you do in the thicket of the Jordan? (Jeremiah 12:5).

Practice of Prayer

Loving Savior, I worry about my job—about whether I'm the best person to do it, if I'll be able to keep it, or if my employer will stay solvent. I don't know what I would do without this job. I don't know how I would pay the bills or take care of my family or even keep my house or apartment. I need this job. At least, that's what I feel, and that's what I believe. But Your Word tells me differently. Your Word tells me that You can provide for me in any manner, through any way. You are the One who directs my steps and establishes my plans.

I don't want my job to become an idol, but when I worry about it, that's what it is. I'm putting more faith in my employer than I am in You. So I'm sorry, and I confess my sin. Forgive me, and help me to know and rest in the truth that no one can take from me what You have declared is mine. They may be smarter, faster, even look more professional—but if this job is the act of service that You have given to me, it will remain mine. Because Your favor will cover my back and guide me to produce effective results. As I depend on You, asking You to help me do my job the best that I possibly can—You will strengthen me to do just that.

And Lord, if I am in a season where You are seeking to transition me to something better—help me not to lose confidence in You. Rather, help me to trust in You, hear clearly from You, and follow You wherever You lead. In Your name, amen.

Personal Prayer Thoughts, Answers, and Reminders

_____

_____

_____

_____

_____

_____

_____

_____

_____

_____

_____

_____

_____

_____

_____

_____

_____

_____

_____

_____

_____

_____

_____

_____

_____

_____

_____

_____

_____

_____

_____

_____

_____

_____

_____

_____

_____

_____

_____

_____

5

Personal Safety

Preparing Our Hearts for Prayer

Worry and concern about personal safety is at an all-time high. Just a cursory glance at social media, online media, or the news can send shivers down anyone's spine. It seems that more so than ever, our culture is rapidly disintegrating as we have left God's protective standards of life.

Did you know that after the 9/11 attacks, Post-Traumatic Stress Disorder (PTSD) increased? Tens of millions witnessed the events on television and online, resulting in a spike. A study was conducted to determine any connection between viewing violence and media reports and individuals suffering from PTSD. This study reported that an increase in concern over our nation's future as well as a decrease in overall confidence in our nation's ability to protect its citizens led to a higher than normal incidence of anxiety and PTSD.[2] Continual exposure to random acts of public violence, home invasions, terrorism threats, and car accidents on our news and social media channels can cause many of us to worry. When we internalize negative and threatening stimuli, they can produce serious and long-lasting neurological effects.

But what would you think if I told you that crime is the lowest it has been in our country since 1970? It is. In fact, violent crime has dropped 51 percent since 1991, and home invasions are down 43 percent.[3] And what would you think if I said motor vehicle deaths are the lowest they have been since 1960? They are. There were fewer fatalities last year than in 1960 on the roads, even though the population on those roads has more than doubled. Because media focuses on violence and localized disasters to stimulate further viewership, we assume that our society is in the worst condition in our lifetimes.

While our exposure to personal safety concerns has skyrocketed due to the Internet and the 24-hour news cycle, the actual risks of danger to our personal safety have greatly decreased over the last two decades. Therefore, one way to overcome worry and anxiety about issues of personal safety is simply to reduce or remove your exposure to it through news and online media. Multiple people have reported a reduction in personal anxiety when they simply stopped watching the news.

Another antidote is to replace your Internet and news time with prayer and thoughts on God's sovereign control. His Word promises us that He is with us wherever we go, and it is God Himself who causes us to lie down, sleep well, and dwell in safety. Wisdom calls to us from the book of Proverbs instructing us that if we listen to wisdom, we will live securely and be at ease from the dread of evil. One of the greatest pieces of wisdom is found in Philippians 4:8: "Finally, brethren, whatever is true, whatever is honorable, whatever is right, whatever is pure, whatever is lovely, whatever is of good repute, if there is any excellence and if anything worthy of praise, dwell on these things."

Set your mind on what is pure, excellent, and praiseworthy, and you will automatically experience a reduction in worry and anxiety over personal safety. This will require personal discipline to refrain from engaging your mind in the disasters of our day, but it is a step toward living free from anxious thoughts regarding potential dangers.

Pursuing God's Presence in Prayer

> Have I not commanded you? Be strong and courageous! Do not tremble or be dismayed, for the LORD your God is with you wherever you go (Joshua 1:9).

> In peace I will both lie down and sleep, for You alone, O LORD, make me to dwell in safety (Psalm 4:8).

> He who listens to me shall live securely and will be at ease from the dread of evil (Proverbs 1:33).

Practice of Prayer

Lord, You have commanded me to be strong and courageous. You have told me not to tremble or be dismayed because You are with me wherever I go. Your angels surround me lest I strike my foot upon a rock. Nothing comes to me to harm me or affect me without having to pass through Your hand of sovereign control. Help me to believe these truths as more than words on paper. Help me to fully believe them and live by them so I am not consumed with worry or anxiety about dangers that could happen.

Regulate my physical body and emotions in such a way that I'm balanced and not given to thoughts of paranoia or fear. Give me wisdom on what to eat, what not to eat, and how to take care of my body and mind so that I live with the greatest physical ability to overcome worry and anxiety. I ask for Your wisdom on what to allow into my mind, and Your strength of self-discipline to not give in to influences that will cause me fear. Set me free from all nightmares and thoughts that disturb my sleep. I will sleep in peace, for You alone make me dwell in safety. In Your name, amen.

Personal Prayer Thoughts, Answers, and Reminders

_____

_____

_____

_____

_____

_____

_____

_____

_____

_____

_____

_____

_____

_____

_____

_____

_____

_____

_____

_____

6

Aging

Preparing Our Hearts for Prayer

Do you recall how you felt about "time" as a teenager? I bet you couldn't wait to grow up to be an adult. Most teens can't. Then there were the college or start-up years when we couldn't wait to meet that "special person" and find the perfect job just waiting for us.

Then somewhere along the line, Father Time started ticking more quickly—or so it felt. Before we knew it, weeks felt like days and years felt like months. If we weren't careful to look up, an entire year could fly by without so much as us even noticing. Aging has a way of making us age even more quickly than we knew possible.

It could be similar to the phenomenon that happens to most of us when we take a road trip. Driving *to* the destination can seem rather long, but the drive home nearly always feels faster. Maybe the allure of the unknown helps our senses to process things more slowly. There really hasn't been a valid scientific reason to explain why this happens! Regardless, the drive back to familiarity seems to be the fastest drive of all.

Perhaps as we move into our twilight years, when predictability becomes more common than not, the clock ticks more quickly for a similar reason. We're heading home.

So if we can't stop aging, how do we at least slow down our thoughts when it comes to worrying about the myriad issues that can come with it? Issues such as:

> What will happen to me if I get sick and no one is there to take care of me?
>
> Will my retirement really pay my bills?
>
> Will my savings allow me to do anything fun, or will I be doomed to watch TV for the rest of my days?
>
> Will my children forget about me, and will I become merely a duty for them to fulfill?
>
> What will I leave my children and grandchildren, and will they make it without me?
>
> Have I even accomplished my purpose in life, or is it too late to dream?
>
> Why do my skin, my face, and my body no longer look like my own?
>
> Is that yet another ache, lump, or strain? What does this one mean? I'm so tired of doctors.
>
> I used to be able to sleep. How do I go through my days without much sleep?
>
> Will I be alone?
>
> Did I make a difference, or will my regrets always rage at my heart?

Aging can be one of the most feared processes for some of us. Thus, the antidote to anxious thoughts about aging can be found in God and His Word. Something so challenging to overcome must be taken to the throne of grace, where we receive mercies to help in times of need. But Paul and Caleb also remind us in the Scriptures that our latter days can actually be greater than our former, if we will but push forward in faith and fear of the Lord.

Pursuing God's Presence in Prayer

> Behold, the LORD has let me live, just as He spoke, these forty-five years, from the time that the LORD spoke this word to Moses, when Israel walked in the wilderness; and now behold, I am eighty-five years old today. I am still as strong today as I was in the day Moses sent me; as my strength was then, so my strength is now, for war and for going out and coming in. Now then, give me this hill country about which the LORD spoke on that day (Joshua 14:10-12).

> We do not lose heart, but though our outer man is decaying, yet our inner man is being renewed day by day (2 Corinthians 4:16).

> Charm is deceitful and beauty is vain, but a woman who fears the LORD, she shall be praised (Proverbs 31:30).

Practice of Prayer

Gracious God who knows the end from the beginning, You do not change, and Your days know no completion. Have compassion on me as I am but human, and my heart often fears this process we call aging. The questions in my mind can scream for answers, but only time can answer them. Thus, I worry, and my thoughts grow anxious inside. Remind me daily of Your consistency and unchanging ways. Give me glimpses of Your faithfulness as I continue in this process of change. Calm my fears as I cast them onto You—fears of the unknown, loss, loneliness, and helplessness—even pain.

Surround me with songs of Your care and Your comfort. Though my outer shell is decaying, my inner self is being renewed day by day. I am renewed and made fresh in Your presence. I am given strength and dignity by fearing You. If Caleb could wait 45 years before pursuing his dream of conquering his part of the Promised Land, then perhaps it's not too late for my dream! Reignite in me my dreams, and give me wisdom on how to pursue them even as I age. I will never be alone as long as I have You. My circumstances and surroundings may change, but Your presence is my guiding light and an ever-present help in times of need. I trust You, Lord, and that trust calms my fears of aging. In Christ's name, amen.

Personal Prayer Thoughts, Answers, and Reminders

_____

_____

_____

_____

_____

_____

_____

_____

_____

_____

_____

_____

_____

_____

_____

_____

_____

_____

_____

_____

_____

7

Future

Preparing Our Hearts for Prayer

Anxiety about the future can cover a plethora of things. We can feel anxious about our financial future, our health, our purpose, our spouse and parents, our children and grandkids, the state of our nation, our safety, our job, our relationships, or even our appearance. The list of things to worry about in the future is endless. But one word sums them all up: *uncertainty*. There is something we all have in common, and that is an inability to predict the future. We can plan. We can anticipate. We can even worry. But none of that will have the final say on what tomorrow will be like. Why not write this verse on a card and stick it on your bathroom mirror? Or on the dashboard of your car? Place it somewhere you'll see it often, so you can relax in the fact that God holds your future and works everything together for your good!

> *You do not know what your life will be like tomorrow.*
> —James 4:14

At the end of the day, we simply cannot know what our lives will be like tomorrow. It's not within our capacity as fallible human beings. But God has not left us here alone. He knows our form and our fears. What's more, He knows our future. And since He does, wouldn't it be the wisest thing of all to draw close to the One who knows the answer to what we may be anxious about? He is our peace as we set our minds on Him. His Word is our guide. His loving-kindness never ceases, and His compassions never fail. They are new every morning, which means there is one thing we can be certain of: God's compassion and loving-kindness will be there to greet us and meet us every step of the way. That truth alone provides solace to the tensions that linger about our unknown tomorrows.

Why is it important to overcome your worries and anxieties about the future? Because these worries and anxieties are stealing the life you have in the present. You cannot predict the future. Neither can you control it. But what you can do is diminish the peace, joy, happiness, and life you have been given today when your mind stays stuck in fearing the unknowns of tomorrow.

God has promised to never leave you. You may not know what the future holds, but you know Who holds the future. Therefore, rest in the power of His intimate presence and grace. God knows the plans He has for you. These are plans for your well-being and not for calamity, to give you a future, and to give you a hope. Try not to muddy today by forgetting these truths about tomorrow.

Pursuing God's Presence in Prayer

> "I know the plans that I have for you," declares the LORD, "plans for welfare and not for calamity to give you a future and a hope" (Jeremiah 29:11).

> Those who wait for the LORD will gain new strength; they will mount up with wings like eagles, they will run and not get tired, they will walk and not become weary (Isaiah 40:31).

This I recall to my mind, therefore I have hope. The
LORD's lovingkindnesses indeed never cease, for His
compassions never fail. They are new every morning;
great is Your faithfulness (Lamentations 3:21-23).

Practice of Prayer

All-knowing God, You have already been in my tomorrow.
You know the end from the beginning. You know what happens
tomorrow. You've seen me smile tomorrow. You've wiped my
tears to come. You already know what is to come. Yet, at times,
I forget how wonderfully good You are and start to worry about
the uncertainty of my tomorrow. I don't want to, but anxious
thoughts can consume me. Forgive my lack of faith in Your loving sovereignty. That's what my worry and anxiety about the
future reveals. If I fully trusted You, I would rest in You and Your
plan for all my tomorrows. Have mercy on me for wanting—
no, *needing*—to know everything in advance. For needing to
be in control. You, oh Lord, are in control, and Your compassions are new every morning.

Help me face my days ahead with the freedom that the birds
face theirs. They neither toil nor grow weary. They do not run
about trying to figure out what to be, do, or eat tomorrow. They
simply rest in knowing that what they need will be provided
by You. God, what I need—maybe not what I want, but what
I truly need—will be provided by You in all my tomorrows.
You have promised to provide for me and to work all things
out for good according to Your purpose. I long to be at ease in
the depth of these truths. Help me to do that. Help me to let
go of that which I cannot control so that I can hold tightly to
that which I can—You, this day, this moment. I love You, Lord,
and I thank You for answering my prayers. You are faithful. In
Christ's name, amen.

Personal Prayer Thoughts, Answers, and Reminders

_____

_____

_____

_____

_____

_____

_____

_____

_____

_____

_____

_____

_____

_____

_____

_____

_____

_____

8

Relationships

Preparing Our Hearts for Prayer

Worry and anxiety can be compared to a flashing light you see as you are driving, indicating danger up ahead. A flashing yellow light on the side of the road can help you avoid imminent danger. But in relationships, the dangers you perceive may be based on past events or trauma. The flashing yellow light doesn't always reflect reality. No matter if they're going well or going badly, relationships provide plenty of opportunity for worry or stress. There are several ways people respond to relationship anxiety:

1. Some people create situations where they can become angry. It is easier to burst into anger than to live in a constant state of worry for them. So they actually look for things to become angry about. Some people make them up subconsciously.

2. Other people choose to give up hope and connection in the relationship. They can become depressed and isolated as a result. To them, living in isolation poses less risk than staying engaged and facing a possible problem in the relationship down the road.

3. A third personality type will try and mask anxiety

and worry about their relationship by turning to coping mechanisms or distractions. Examples include: overworking, overspending, drinking alcohol, binge-watching TV, and other obsessive behaviors.

Anxiety about a relationship is the fastest way to actually ruin the relationship. Fears dominate conversations when you worry, making it difficult to work toward solutions for actual problems when they arise. Suspicion and worry about things that "may" happen can contribute to a major relationship breakdown. Focusing negatively on the future can deeply damage the present.

The antidote for worry and anxiety about relationships rests in trust. Not necessarily trust in the other person, but rather trust in a sovereign God who has your best interests at heart when you are committed to Him. People may let you down in relationships, but when your heart accepts that God has a plan for everything that happens to you, you can look for the way to be a blessing in the midst of burdens.

Scripture tells us that love always trusts. To worry and become anxious about things in a relationship is in direct violation of that biblical command to love. Essentially, it is sinning. To sin will invite destruction and negative consequences into any relationship. Instead, put your hope in God—taking the risk to love in light of His overarching care for you. Then watch Him usher in blessing where there previously was only worry. God rewards your actions and thoughts done in faith.

Pursuing God's Presence in Prayer

He who walks with wise men will be wise, but the companion of fools will suffer harm (Proverbs 13:20).

Let us consider how to stimulate one another to love and good deeds, not forsaking our own assembling together, as is the habit of some, but encouraging one another; and all the more as you see the day drawing near (Hebrews 10:24-25).

With all humility and gentleness, with patience, showing tolerance for one another in love, being diligent to preserve the unity of the Spirit in the bond of peace (Ephesians 4:2-3).

Practice of Prayer

Lord Jesus, You have told us that the two greatest commandments are to love God and to love others. You've also given us the description of what love is—and what it isn't—in 1 Corinthians 13. When I am worried or anxious about my relationships, I am not choosing obedience to You. Please forgive me for filling my heart and mind with the opposite of faith. Love always trusts, even if the person and situation is untrustworthy. This is because when I follow You in faith, You will cover me with protection, compassion, and care.

Lord, I ask that You will make me a blessing to those around me. Make me a model of what love really looks like. Allow my interaction with those I love to encourage them to live at a higher level of love themselves. Let my spirit, words, and thoughts be filled with humility, gentleness, patience, and tolerance. May I be truly diligent to preserve the unity of the Spirit in the bond of peace. In Christ's name, amen.

Personal Prayer Thoughts, Answers, and Reminders

_____

_____

_____

_____

_____

_____

_____

_____

_____

_____

_____

_____

_____

_____

_____

_____

_____

_____

_____

_____

9

What We Eat

Preparing Our Hearts for Prayer

Food used to be a simple choice to make. There was a time when we weren't faced with a myriad of options from non-GMO to organic to gluten-free to vegan to…you name it. I'm sure that tomorrow there will be something new to choose. What's worse is that one year we are told that bacon is bad for you, and a few years later, it's not. Or one decade we're told to drink juice all day—*it's not just for breakfast anymore*—and then a decade later we discover the spike juice has on insulin levels, making it no longer advisable even for breakfast anymore.

Researching about what to eat, where to eat, when to eat, how to eat, and how to prepare food is enough to be a full-time job. Worrying about these things can be just as intensive, if not more.

So what can we do as we determine our eating choices and help influence the choices of those under our care? First and foremost, we must consecrate the activity of eating before God. First Corinthians 10:31 makes it clear: "Whether, then, you eat or drink or whatever you do, do all to the glory of God." Thus, what we put into our bodies should be put there with the intention of bringing glory to God. After all, our bodies are not our own—they were purchased by Christ on the cross

(1 Corinthians 6:19). That extra donut or that pizza buffet might not be the wisest choice for the "temple of the Holy Spirit." An unhealthy consumption of sugar and processed foods has been linked to poor mental health, proving that eating and emotions can go hand in hand. In fact, long-term intake of unhealthy foods has been linked to both depression and increases in anxiety.

So if you are anxious about what you eat and how it affects your body, you'll want to start by passing your food choices through a grid: Will this food choice enable me to bring glory to God? By asking that, you are choosing foods that provide you with the necessary nutrients, vitamins, carbohydrates, and healthy fats needed for all the billions—yes, that's billions with a *b*—of neurons in your brain alone. Scientists estimate there are more neurons in your entire body than there are stars in the Milky Way. That should keep us from eating too many Milky Ways and other candy bars!

Worrying about food should be constructively turned into efforts toward making good eating choices. But after that, any worry or anxiety needs to be turned over to God. Scripture says that your life is more than food. We are directly told not to worry about our lives, as to what we will eat or drink. Rather, we are to nourish our bodies with what God has provided and place our trust in Him—the maker, preserver, and sustainer of all things.

Pursuing God's Presence in Prayer

> I say to you, do not be worried about your life, as to what you will eat or what you will drink; nor for your body, as to what you will put on. Is not life more than food, and the body more than clothing? (Matthew 6:25).

> Whether, then, you eat or drink or whatever you
> do, do all to the glory of God (1 Corinthians 10:31).

> I encourage you to take some food, for this is for
> your preservation (Acts 27:34).

Practice of Prayer

Loving Father, You have provided us with so many wonderful things to eat. The creativity and delight You have put into the creation of food for us is beyond comprehension. Thank You for making so many options to delight our taste buds and satisfy our hunger.

Lord, because a lot of harmful things go into the processing and preparation of foods these days, I ask that You will please cover me and my loved ones with Your protective care. Shield us from any spoiled food or bacteria. Guard our bodies from the negative impact of processed breads and sugars. Give us the self-control we need to make healthy food choices. I want my mind to be sharp and my energy levels to be high, so please give me wisdom on what food to eat—and what to avoid—in order to make this possible.

As for the unseen germs and issues lurking in foods I might consume, I ask for Your mercies of protection—enabling my body to detoxify and remain healthy. Father, I also ask that You will give me the grace of peace and assurance, so that I will not worry but rather commit the very act of enjoying the food You have created for Your glory. In Christ's name, amen.

Personal Prayer Thoughts, Answers, and Reminders

_____

_____

_____

_____

_____

_____

_____

_____

_____

_____

_____

_____

_____

_____

_____

_____

_____

_____

_____

_____

10

Diseases and Sickness

Preparing Our Hearts for Prayer

Health anxiety, otherwise known in some fields as illness anxiety disorder, is the preoccupation with potential health issues our bodies may be experiencing or could one day experience. This is different from the worry and anxiety we may feel when we, or a loved one, is struggling with a diagnosed disease or chronic sickness. These worries stem from the concern of what our bodies may be facing, dealing with, or suffering from. Legitimate concern and difficulties that arise from chronic illnesses and disease can impact us deeply.

Nearly half of all Americans suffer from a chronic illness. Statistics tell us that 75 percent of all marriages that have a major chronic illness or disease introduced into the relationship after the marriage took place will likely end in divorce.[4] The daily strain of anxiety, health management, and uncertainty attached to disease and chronic illness is often more than people can bear—or bear well.

Healing and health are coveted commodities in today's world. And the Lord has a lot to say about these topics in His Word. When healing is to be granted, we can seek it through prayer offered in faith. Healing comes first and foremost from God, so looking to Him in our times of trial is our greatest priority. Calling out to Him in prayer for healing is a productive use of our energy, whereas worrying is not. God holds the future in His hands. There is no one greater or more powerful to turn to when our bodies suffer from serious disease.

But there are times when healing isn't immediate or forthcoming. God's ways are different from our own, and sickness, disease, and chronic health issues are a part of living in a sinful world. While we wait on the possibility for healing, there are some things we can do to ease the suffering of worry and anxiety. We can start by applying the wisdom of Proverbs 16:24, which teaches us that "pleasant words are a honeycomb, sweet to the soul and healing to the bones." Did you know that your words can affect your health? They can. What you think and what you speak have the power to tear down or build up. Proverbs 18:21 tells us that the power of life and death are in the tongue. Constant talk and continual thoughts of what could go wrong, what is going wrong, what hurts, and what struggles you are facing simply breed more of the same. One of the most important approaches to good health is speaking positively about your life, health, vitality, strength, and healing. Your words matter, as do your thoughts.

Another thing you can do when suffering from disease or chronic illness is to write down your list of worries. After you've written out your worries, divide them into "productive worries" and "unproductive worries." Productive worries are those you can do something about. If you can do something about it, then do it. If you can't, you'll need to move it to the "unproductive worries" column by casting that worry onto the Lord and leaving it with Him. When you are suffering from a disease or chronic illness, you don't have excess energy to spend on worry and anxiety. You must exercise personal discipline to give your unproductive worries to God, or you will only wear yourself down further.

In addition to giving your worries to the Lord, learn how to embrace uncertainty. Embracing uncertainty is a life skill that will enable you to cherish and be present in the now. Rather than living in the *what-ifs* of the future, you can choose to live in the *what-is* right now. This is an approach to life that even people without disease or chronic illness should practice. Too often we miss out on our lives because we are constantly living in the future or the past rather than experiencing the present—which is all we truly have. Let this disease or chronic illness teach this all-important lesson of being present, aware, and grateful. When you live one day at a time, you will discover that the things that overwhelmed and caused you anxiety don't have nearly as much power as they did before.

Lastly, laugh and cry. Worry and anxiety suppress the amygdala—the part of the brain that houses our emotions. When you allow or even encourage yourself to laugh or cry, you are giving life to your emotions and lessening your own ability to worry or feel anxious. Watch movies or videos that make you laugh. Seek out people and activities that will give your mind something to engage with on a positive nature. And know that, despite any prognosis you may be facing for yourself or a loved one, you know the Great Physician. He is able to do exceedingly above all we could ever ask or imagine. Ask for healing while trusting Him in the waiting period.

Pursuing God's Presence in Prayer

> The prayer offered in faith will restore the one who is sick, and the Lord will raise him up, and if he has committed sins, they will be forgiven him (James 5:15).

> Bless the LORD, O my soul, and forget none of His

benefits; who pardons all your iniquities, who heals all your diseases (Psalm 103:2-3).

Pleasant words are a honeycomb, sweet to the soul and healing to the bones (Proverbs 16:24).

Practice of Prayer

Great Healer, my God—You have made my body. You created my being. You formed me when I was in my mother's womb. You know what it takes for me to live a healthy, full life. Yet I am faced with this disease or chronic illness. It limits my ability to focus and to carry out all of the things my heart desires. Teach me in this time of testing to depend solely on You. Give me wisdom on how my body has been made and how it functions best, so that I will choose the right things to give it: minerals, vitamins, food, rest, laughter, and more. Show me where I am contributing to my poor health either through worry, anxiety, or other poor choices, and give me the courage and willpower to stop.

Lord, I want to be healed. I want to be completely whole. So I ask for Your healing hand with my whole heart. Yet, Lord, if You have chosen to allow this infirmity for whatever reason, give me the grace to manage it well. Let it not negatively impact my relationships; rather, let it improve them. Let it not negatively impact my attitudes, work, or purpose; rather, let it give them depth and richness. Let this season be my teacher and guide, strengthening my soul and drawing me closer to You. I cannot control what my body does and how it responds to treatments or approaches, but I can control what my mind thinks; and I choose to think thoughts of life, wholeness, health, and joy. I am whole in Christ. In His name, amen.

Personal Prayer Thoughts, Answers, and Reminders

_____

_____

_____

_____

_____

_____

_____

_____

_____

_____

_____

_____

_____

_____

_____

_____

_____

_____

_____

_____

_____

_____

_____

_____

_____

_____

_____

_____

_____

_____

_____

_____

_____

_____

_____

_____

_____

_____

_____

_____

_____

_____

_____

God's Acceptance

Preparing Our Hearts for Prayer

Jesus loves me" is a song we've all sung at some point in our lives. We've probably led others in singing it too—maybe our kids or nieces or nephews. The words of the song are simple but powerful: "Yes, Jesus loves me…the Bible tells me so." And for most of us, that's easy enough to swallow. After all, He did die on the cross for our sins.

But does Jesus *like* me? Or does God, for that matter? Far too many of us wonder whether or not God really does *like* us. Yes, we know He loves us, but would He spend time with us if given the chance? Would He walk across the room and sit down at our lunch table? Does God get bored during our prayers? Is He pretty much disappointed in all that we do? God's acceptance of us goes much deeper than love. We worry whether or not He truly accepts us for who we are. The problems arise when we feel that He doesn't accept us—when we avoid Him as we would avoid someone we felt we could never please. After all, who wants to spend time with someone they are convinced doesn't like them at all? No one. That is why it is so important that we understand the content and scope of God's love. In it we discover that He truly does like us as well.

God loves us deeply, even though He may not be pleased by

our sinful choices or attitudes. When that occurs, however, He doesn't reject us personally. Rather, as our heavenly Father, He tenderly disciplines us back to right living (Hebrews 12:5-6). God accepts us wholeheartedly because of the substitutionary death of Christ on our behalf, even when we lived in rebellion against Him (Ephesians 1:4-5). God adopted us into His family and gave us the most precious gift: the forgiveness of our sins through the death of Christ.

His death frees us from the fear of rejection that sin evokes. When we fail to embrace and accept Christ's atonement for our sins (not just for eternity but also for our everyday life), we are asserting that His death wasn't quite good enough.

Christ's death was good enough—not only to get us into heaven, but also to provide us with the acceptance we need to live vibrantly here on earth. Acceptance from God is not a thing He's dangling in front of us like a carrot we will never reach. Acceptance from God comes from His heart of pure love.

God's gift is one of the more difficult things we as believers can accept. Guilt, shame, and regret stand in the way of our believing it. The antidote to worry or anxiety over God's acceptance of you is Jesus Himself. He died, was raised, and is at the right hand of God, interceding for you, accepting you, and declaring boldly that there is no condemnation for you when you simply abide in Him. He guarantees it, too, with His life. The love and acceptance of God toward His children is unconditional—and therefore, there's no need to worry or be anxious about whether He loves you. His heart is always open to you.

Pursuing God's Presence in Prayer

> Who is the one who condemns? Christ Jesus is
> He who died, yes, rather who was raised, who is at

the right hand of God, who also intercedes for us
(Romans 8:34).

Accept one another, just as Christ also accepted us
to the glory of God (Romans 15:7).

Therefore there is now no condemnation for those
who are in Christ Jesus (Romans 8:1).

Practice of Prayer

Lord, humbly I come to You in prayer, acknowledging the
power of Christ's love and redemption. I know my sins and my
shortcomings, God, and how I deserve the consequences of
what I've done—including a break in my fellowship with You.
But Your Word tells me that I am not condemned when I am in
Christ Jesus. I am fully accepted, loved, cherished, and adored
by You. Thank You for loving me so fully. Thank You for Your
ability to forgive and release the pains I have caused You and
those You also love. Thank You for giving me grace and mercy
time and time again.

When I worry that I am not good enough to be on Your
"good side," point me to the cross. Point me to the ultimate price
that was paid to secure my acceptance with You. Help me not to
make light of that payment by shrinking back at what You are
giving to me—Your love, Your grace, Your pleasure, and Your
promises. I am accepted by You, fully and freely. May my life
choices reflect that truth, and may my heart resonate with the
peace Your love supplies. In Christ's name, amen.

Personal Prayer Thoughts, Answers, and Reminders

_____

_____

_____

_____

_____

_____

_____

_____

_____

_____

_____

_____

_____

_____

_____

_____

_____

_____

_____

National Security

Preparing Our Hearts for Prayer

In an increasingly global economy and society, national security has managed to move up on our awareness radar. Not that it was ever low. As a whole, fears of nuclear war and national attack have plagued us for decades. The threat of terrorism has only led to an increase in what many already fear. A recent poll published in the *Washington Post* revealed that 83 percent of registered voters in America believed a serious terrorist attack would happen again in their lifetime.[5] That's nearly all of us.

When presidential debates occur, national security is a key point of discussion. While we carry this worry around with us, things like elections bring this concern to the forefront of many minds. And rightfully so. Our nation, like all nations, is vulnerable to attack. That's why in overcoming worry and anxiety concerning national security, we must go straight to the Captain of the Lord's army—Christ Himself. "The earth is the LORD's, and all it contains" (Psalm 24:1). When we lose sight of that truth, worry can consume us.

We may think that the American people carry the full authority to choose our leaders, or that world leaders are put there by chance. But Scripture tells us otherwise: "It is He who changes the times and the epochs; He removes kings and establishes kings" (Daniel 2:21). We also read, "The king's heart is like channels of water in the hand of the LORD; He turns it wherever He wishes" (Proverbs 21:1). We may think that man is in control, but God is in ultimate control. And because God's plan and perspective are much broader than ours, He will frequently allow things to happen that make no sense to us from our very limited perspective. Who can comprehend the mind of God? "'For My thoughts are not your thoughts, nor are your ways My ways,' declares the LORD. 'For as the heavens are higher than the earth, so are My ways higher than your ways and My thoughts than your thoughts'" (Isaiah 55:8-9).

It is only when we surrender to the truth that "God reigns over the nations, God sits on His holy throne" (Psalm 47:8), that we will discover the ability to turn our worries and cares about our nation to Him. Worry is an affront to the One in control, as it reveals our doubts that He really is who He says He is. Surrendering and abandoning our fears about our nation is an act of obedience and faith to the King of kings and ruler of all nations. No, His choices don't always make sense to us, and our world is not a peaceful utopia, but as a child of the King, you can rest knowing that peace is *your* rightful claim when you align your thoughts with His truth.

Pursuing God's Presence in Prayer

> May peace be within your walls, and prosperity within your palaces (Psalm 122:7).

> The LORD bless you from Zion, and may you see the prosperity of Jerusalem all the days of your life. Indeed, may you see your children's children (Psalm 128:5-6).

> Behold, I will bring to it health and healing, and I

will heal them; and I will reveal to them an abundance of peace and truth (Jeremiah 33:6).

Practice of Prayer

King of kings and Lord of lords, I come to You today with a heart full of anxious thoughts about our national security. So many things can go wrong, God, and national disaster can happen in an instant. Lord, I want to be free from worry and anxiety, so I look to You as my strength and source for peace. Your Word tells me that You truly are in control, despite how things appear. Your Word tells me that You sit in authority over all nations. Nothing can happen to us that doesn't first pass through Your kind and powerful hand of sovereignty.

Remind me of these truths when thoughts creep into my mind that say otherwise. Despite the chaos around us, You are the calm within. When I lack trust in our national leaders, I am reminded that their choices are not made without Your overarching governance. Their choices may be wrong, unwise, wicked, or foolish—but You have never been One who relies on conventional means to deliver Your people from national threats. Look at Jericho. Look at the Red Sea. Look at David pretending to be a madman. Help me to focus less on what I see and more on who I know: You. Less on the means and more on the Master. In Christ's name, I trust You—amen.

Personal Prayer Thoughts, Answers, and Reminders

_____

_____

_____

_____

_____

_____

_____

_____

_____

_____

_____

_____

_____

_____

_____

_____

_____

_____

_____

_____

13

Personal Value

Preparing Our Hearts for Prayer

Personal value is not to be confused with self-esteem or feelings of significance. While both of the latter weigh heavily on performance, personal value rests more deeply within. Our sense of personal value can be hindered by feelings of shame, guilt, and regret. These three things can destroy a mind's perception of personal value, sometimes instantaneously.

Our enemy likes nothing more than increasing our feelings of shame and guilt because those emotions drive us from the presence of God. They don't drive God from us, but rather us from Him. Take for example Adam and Eve in the garden. You can recall what they did when their eyes were opened and they realized their nakedness. This man and woman, in their shame, literally tried to hide from God.

There are many reasons why we would try to hide from God in the midst of shame, guilt, and regret. One of those reasons is because we may feel He doesn't love us anymore. Another is that we fear the consequences we intuitively know come tied to the things that cause shame and guilt. A third reason we seek to hide from the Lord is illustrated by the prophet Isaiah, who stood before God in His throne room and mouthed the words, "Woe is me, for I am ruined! Because I am a man of unclean lips, and I live among a people of unclean lips; for my eyes have seen the King, the LORD of hosts" (Isaiah 6:5). We hide because of God's holiness.

Imagine walking into a five-star restaurant in your gym pants and sweaty shirt. You would most likely make a run for the bathroom to change. Why? Because the standard of dress all around you would be too much to endure. You would either want to meet that standard or shrink back from it. Thus, when we as sinners come face-to-face with our own shame, guilt, and regret, and then likewise come face-to-face with God's ultimate purity, the two don't mix. A sparkling diamond always looks brightest against a black backdrop, and God's holiness appears even more stark compared to us when we are acutely aware of our own lack.

On our own, though—just like Isaiah—we will never be able to clean up enough to remove shame, guilt, and regret. In Isaiah's situation, an angel flew to him with coal from the altar of the Lord. Then the angel touched Isaiah's lips with it and declared, "Behold, this has touched your lips; and your iniquity is taken away and your sin is forgiven" (Isaiah 6:7). Only after receiving God's forgiveness can we overcome worry and anxiety about our personal value.

Truth is, we will never be pure enough, clean enough, honest enough, sinless enough, or you-name-it enough without God's help and forgiveness. Yes, some of our sin caused feelings of shame and guilt, and some of our shame is due to other sinners. Regardless, forgiveness is required to reach a level of personal value in our own hearts. Your value is intrinsically tied to Christ Himself, and the grace He has provided. His death, burial, and resurrection declare you a child of the King, and royal blood runs through your veins. Memorize this and say it each day: "He made Him who knew no sin to be sin on our behalf, so that we might become the righteousness of God in Him" (2 Corinthians 5:21). You *are* the righteousness of God in Christ. Christ is in you, the hope of glory, which gives you exquisite personal value.

Pursuing God's Presence in Prayer

> You formed my inward parts; You wove me in my mother's womb. I will give thanks to You, for I am fearfully and wonderfully made; wonderful are Your works, and my soul knows it very well. My frame was not hidden from You, when I was made in secret (Psalm 139:13-15).

> Are not five sparrows sold for two cents? Yet not one of them is forgotten before God. Indeed, the very hairs of your head are all numbered. Do not fear; you are more valuable than many sparrows (Luke 12:6-7).

> You are a chosen race, a royal priesthood, a holy nation, a people for God's own possession, so that you may proclaim the excellencies of Him who has called you out of darkness into His marvelous light (1 Peter 2:9).

Practice of Prayer

Blessed Lord, I am a chosen person, a member of the royal priesthood, declared and created by You for Your own possession. You have placed me here to proclaim the perfection and beauty of who You are. You have called me out of darkness and into Your marvelous light. You have sought me where I was hiding and asked me to stand boldly at Your throne of grace. You have given me fresh clothes, washed in Christ's love. I am valuable to You. I am valuable to me. I am valuable to others around me. You have gifted me by creating me in the image of Yourself, complete with the ability and capacity to love, encourage, edify, and strengthen others.

Open my eyes to my worth, Lord. Remove the feelings and emotions of shame, guilt, and regret. I am not condemned when I am in Christ Jesus. I walk freely with my head held high, with royal blood flowing in my veins. I am a child of the King. I am royalty. I am whole, well, emotionally stable, loving, kind, generous, giving, trusting, and lovable. Let me walk in that truth each and every day. Defend me from the fiery darts that Satan throws my way. Replace them with the compassions of Christ, in which I feel fully alive. In Christ's name, amen.

Personal Prayer Thoughts, Answers, and Reminders

_____

_____

_____

_____

_____

_____

_____

_____

_____

_____

_____

_____

_____

_____

_____

_____

_____

_____

_____

_____

_____

_____

14

Low Energy Levels

Preparing Our Hearts for Prayer

A low energy level ranks as one of the highest physical complaints of Americans. Some people blame it on multitasking or adding too much to our daily schedules. Others blame it on poor eating choices. But did you know that just as important as your eating choices is *how* you eat what you choose? How you eat really matters. Eating quickly or eating while distracted will negatively impact your digestion. Anything that slows down your digestion will decrease your energy as well. Also, while constant multitasking may lead some to experience low energy levels, one of the more frequent contributors to decreased energy comes from something we forget to do when we get busy: breathing deeply.

Sure, we breathe enough to sustain life. I know that is true, or you and I wouldn't be reading these pages right now. But what we often don't do is breathe deeply enough and slowly enough to adequately intake oxygen and deliver it to our cells. Going throughout your day with decreased oxygen in your cells is like trying to drive to work on fumes in your tank. You may sputter around for a mile or two, but you'll eventually come to a stop.

However, worrying about low energy levels and what might be causing them, though, is counterproductive. In fact, a low

99

energy level is the most frequent physical manifestation of anxiety. Why is this? When your body feels worried or anxious, adrenaline comes to the rescue to help you fight off whatever danger you may be facing. When that danger is worry or anxiety, the demand for adrenaline can linger. Because there is nothing to trigger an end to the worry, the demand can put too much effort on your adrenal glands. Just as you get tired after a difficult job or heavy workout, so do your adrenal glands. They do what you probably do after that workout—shut down. Crash. Now, not only can they no longer produce the energy you need, but also you will experience a crash from overusing your limited adrenaline.

Have you ever been driving when a car almost pulled out in front of you at a four-way stop? Or almost hit you? That feeling you have after you realize everything is okay can usually be described as exhaustion. When your body crashes from the adrenaline rush, it is tired. When you worry about many things, or even one thing over and over again, your body is in a constant state of adrenaline rush/crash—on top of your adrenal glands being depleted and worn-out. What is the antidote for low energy levels? Eating healthy foods, increasing certain vitamins, sleeping well (but not too long), and exercising are helpful habits. But the most important antidote is to turn your worries and anxiety over to God. When you no longer have to use your physical body and mental energies to combat negative thoughts, fears, and concerns, your body will have access to the energy God supplied you to handle the daily experiences of life.

Pursuing God's Presence in Prayer

> He gives strength to the weary, and to him who lacks might He increases power (Isaiah 40:29).

> She girds herself with strength and makes her arms strong (Proverbs 31:17).

[You will walk] strengthened with all power, according to His glorious might, for the attaining of all steadfastness and patience (Colossians 1:11).

Practice of Prayer

Lord, You give power to the faint. To those who have no might, You increase their strength. You are my source, but too often I get in the way of accessing Your strength. It is only when I align my thoughts with Your truth that I can let go of worry and anxiety. Your Word promises me that You will keep me in perfect peace when my mind is focused on You (Isaiah 26:3). So Lord, where do I start? How do I let go of the things that cause me to be afraid?

I start by replacing my thoughts with Yours. I start by reading and meditating on Your promises. I start by tearing down strongholds in my mind that cause me to be anxious. *You are in control.* You hold my life and my loved ones in Your hands. Period. No weapon formed against me will prosper. It may form, but Your Word says it will not prosper. You have never let the righteous be forsaken. You have never and will never leave me. I *can* do all things through Christ who gives me strength. Christ gives me strength. When I have no strength, then it is because I am not looking to Christ.

Forgive me and help me to turn my gaze from my fears to You in faith. Give me small victories along the way—stones of remembrance—that I can look to, knowing that You truly are the supplier of all I need, and that Your grace is sufficient for me. In my weakness, You make me strong. Help me meditate on that truth all day long. In Christ's name, amen.

Personal Prayer Thoughts, Answers, and Reminders

_____

_____

_____

_____

_____

_____

_____

_____

_____

_____

_____

_____

_____

_____

_____

_____

_____

_____

_____

_____

15

Loneliness

Preparing Our Hearts for Prayer

Most of us are surrounded by people all of the time. If we are not in the physical proximity of people, we are still connected through emails, texting, calling, and social media. And yet the numbers of people who admit to suffering from loneliness have more than doubled since 1980.[6] Loneliness has nothing to do with the number of friends a person has or even with how many social interactions fill a calendar. Researchers have discovered that loneliness stems from a disconnection between a person's expectations for how relationships are to be and the reality of those relationships. When there is an increase in relational dissatisfaction—whether with a marriage partner, children, friends, coworkers, family, romantic relationships, or others—the effects of loneliness set in.

Several subtle signs that a person might be lonely include: a preoccupation with shopping or purchasing material items; the tendency to take frequent long, hot showers or baths; a fascination with social media sites; weight gain; low immune response; binge-watching TV; and interrupted sleep patterns. Overcoming loneliness is important because the impact of it on our physical

ct, recurring feelings of loneliness have
person's risk of premature death by 14
e amount for obesity.)

ss is very different from being alone.
gs of disconnection from those
leads to frustration and even depression.
Many married couples suffer from loneliness, as do many people who appear to have an active social life. Loneliness stems from a lack of authentic understanding of and appreciation for someone else, and vice versa.

Again, being alone differs from loneliness. This may be surprising, but being alone for periods of time has actually been shown to provide positive impact on a person's mind and body. These include an increase in creativity, reflection, personal analysis, rest, recuperation, feelings of freedom, increased focus, and even improved self-esteem. These benefits often stem from one opportunity that being alone provides, which is to connect fully with God. Jesus made a habit of being alone during His time on earth. In Matthew 4:1-11, He was alone for 40 days in the wilderness. In Matthew 14:23, "He went up on the mountain by Himself to pray." In Mark 1:35, we read that Jesus departed while it was still dark so He could go to a desolate place and commune with God. And in Luke 4:42, Jesus again went to a secluded place to be alone.

Remember, because of God's presence in our lives, being "alone" is never truly alone. You are with God. Hebrews 13:5 reveals one of the most powerful truths in the Bible, seen clearly through its structure in the original Greek language. This short verse—"I will never desert you, nor will I ever forsake you"—contains four different negative Greek words. It is called emphatic negation, and it is the strongest form of Greek negation. In English, two negatives cancel each other out. But in

Greek, they intensify the meaning. Thus, God will never, never, never, never, never leave you. You are not alone even when you are alone.

Far too often, we confuse our fear of loneliness with that of being alone—when in reality, times of solitude have been used for spiritual disciplines throughout the ages. Quiet time with God can provide strength and refreshment. The antidote to loneliness, then, is not about keeping ourselves from being alone, but in the type of relationships we have with other people and with the Lord. Learn to open up to others and enjoy sharing your life with a few close friends. Learn to spend time alone in God's presence, and learn to enjoy Him. When you look to God as your primary source for emotional care, love, protection, and enjoyment, you will also learn better how to love and enjoy others and yourself. Then, when you are with others, expectations for what you each share together will be more meaningful. Try journaling and writing down your feelings just with the Lord—you will find Him a tender listener and an incredible friend. What a Friend we have in Jesus!

Pursuing God's Presence in Prayer

> I will never desert you, nor will I ever forsake you (Hebrews 13:5).

> Your husband is your Maker, whose name is the LORD of hosts; and your Redeemer is the Holy One of Israel, who is called the God of all the earth (Isaiah 54:5).

> A man of too many friends comes to ruin, but there is a friend who sticks closer than a brother (Proverbs 18:24).

Practice of Prayer

Loving Christ, You set an example for me while You were on earth of seeking out solitude as a way of refreshing Your soul and gaining strength. Help me to understand the gift of solitude and to incorporate it meaningfully into my life. Help me to experience the presence of God in such a way that I know I am not alone. Give me wisdom about things and activities I do that increase my feelings of loneliness. If I need to cut back on making comparisons and setting unreal expectations through engaging in social media, give me the self-discipline to do that.

Help me to view myself the way You view me. Help me to gain a greater value for who I am and my connection to You. When I do, I will put less pressure on others to meet the needs You and I are designed to meet in me.

I also ask for increased intimacy and relational authenticity with friends and family. May I know what it is like to be a friend, and to have one. To give love, and to receive it—unconditionally. To care, and to be cared for. To share, and to listen. Lord, You have built us for community, but we have disregarded that community in so many ways. Guide me into relationships that will help form authentic community around me, where I can connect genuinely. In Christ's name, amen.

Personal Prayer Thoughts, Answers, and Reminders

_____

_____

_____

_____

_____

_____

_____

_____

_____

_____

_____

_____

_____

_____

_____

_____

_____

_____

_____

_____

_____

_____

_____

_____

_____

_____

_____

_____

_____

_____

_____

_____

_____

_____

_____

_____

_____

_____

_____

_____

16

Lack of Purpose

Preparing Our Hearts for Prayer

The Bureau of Labor and Statistics recently did a study that mapped out the typical usage of people's days, divided by gender, age, and educational level. However, no matter what the gender, age, or educational level of the person, the chart looked relatively the same. The size of the pieces of pie might have been larger for some—for example, the elderly spent considerably more time watching television than those younger than them—but overall, the pieces of pie were divided along the same lines.

These things included eating, sleeping, household chores, working, time with our family and friends, time with the Lord, worship at our church, caring for others, and leisure or sports. That's the American life in a nutshell—or rather, in a pie. And while those things are important and essential to life, what is missing for too many of us is purpose. Yes, purpose can be found in caring for others, including your family. It can also be found in working. But according to a recent *Forbes* report, 42 percent of employees surveyed had recently left their jobs for another one due to stress.[8] If half of the workplace is up and leaving, that doesn't say much for finding purpose and significance in work.

Questions of purpose plague us from early on, yet so few seem to discover theirs. We ask questions such as: Why am I here? What am I supposed to do? What was I created to fulfill? What is my destiny? These questions sound more loudly than the ticking clock reminding us we are not here forever. Worrying about purpose, though, can have a very damaging effect. Namely, when you give in to worry and anxiety about your purpose, you are likely to miss out on your present. Purpose is important. After all, God "saved us and called us with a holy calling, not according to our works, but according to His own purpose" (2 Timothy 1:9). We each have a "holy calling." But what we often neglect to realize is that calling integrates into our daily life.

Purpose resides in committing your works to the Lord. It is found in whether you eat or drink, doing it all unto God. Purpose exists in your daily choices—in being an authentic friend, family member, or community volunteer; in putting your cell phone down when you go through the checkout line and asking the person in front of you about their day; and in living a life modeled after Jesus, who changed His plans when He was tired and worn-out and chose to feed 5000 instead of sending them away. You may not feed 5000, but you may feed your family— or a friend or even a stranger.

Grand purposes exist, and this is not to say that you shouldn't dream or pursue a great calling. But the antidote for worrying about lacking purpose in your life comes from realizing you may be living your purpose right this very moment. The greatest commandments that we've been given are to love God with all of our heart and to love others as ourselves. Doing so doesn't require a degree, a mission trip, or even a platform. It requires humility, selflessness, and the grace to put God and others first in your life. That is the greatest purpose of them all. And it is something we all can do, whenever and wherever we are. Dream, yes. But never allow your dream to diminish your daily destiny of loving God and loving others. I invite you to join with me in a 12-week course I recently completed on "Dream Again," which can be seen on the brucewilkinson .com website.

Pursuing God's Presence in Prayer

> For this reason I have allowed you to remain, in order to show you My power and in order to proclaim My name through all the earth (Exodus 9:16).

> My beloved, just as you have always obeyed, not as in my presence only, but now much more in my absence, work out your salvation with fear and trembling; for it is God who is at work in you, both to will and to work for His good pleasure (Philippians 2:12-13).

> We are His workmanship, created in Christ Jesus for good works, which God prepared beforehand so that we would walk in them (Ephesians 2:10).

Practice of Prayer

Father, teach me to know Your ways. Guide me with Your love into my holy calling. Help me to recognize the value of each day and how great an impact I can have on those around me. Let me be the one to sow seeds of life through what I say. Grant me the grace to truly listen and to invest in the lives You bring across my path.

I know You have created me to fulfill a unique purpose that will bring other people good, myself pleasure, and You glory. On this path to purpose, I have experienced setbacks, testing, development, and wilderness seasons. These things can tempt me to worry and wonder if I'll ever even get there. But in the midst of that pursuit, God, may I never neglect the daily purpose of loving You and loving others. Delight my heart with the joy of seeing how I can be used by You in the most everyday, mundane aspects of life. That is true purpose, and it's right before my eyes. In Christ's name, amen.

Personal Prayer Thoughts, Answers, and Reminders

_____

_____

_____

_____

_____

_____

_____

_____

_____

_____

_____

_____

_____

_____

_____

_____

_____

_____

_____

_____

_____

_____

17

Economic Collapse

Preparing Our Hearts for Prayer

The impact of economic collapse on mental health has been examined for a century. Suicide rates increased from 12 per 100,000 prior to the Great Depression up to 19 per 100,000 during the 11-year slump. When the stock market crashed as recently as 2008, a phenomenon known as "recession depression" began to impact people, whether they had lost their homes or not. Because of the housing crisis, layoffs and cutbacks increased in businesses, and a general uncertainty about national economic health filtered through almost everything.

Worry and anxiety regarding something as out of our immediate control as an economic collapse affects all of us. We are concerned about providing for a family, paying for children's quality education, reducing debt, and living securely—especially when threats of economic collapse hit the news. So how do we overcome the temptation to worry about the overall financial status of our nation and its impact on our own lives? Primarily by recognizing that God is the sovereign ruler over all. Despite how things may appear, God is in control. Both riches and honor come from Him, and He rules over all. That means when riches and honor are hard to come by, such as in a time of economic downturn, God has chosen to allow a season of want and lack. His hands hold both power and might, even when we do not understand His reasons.

Realizing that God is able to provide—even in times of economic collapse—can also help alleviate the fear of not knowing what to do if our money runs out. The prophet Elijah sat starving by a brook after running miles for his life, yet God was faithful to provide for him by commanding the ravens to bring him food. Every morning and every night, the Lord used a bird to provide for His servant. God isn't limited by human means when it comes to providing. In fact, He can go outside of His own parameters, as He did when using a raven—a bird He had previously declared unclean—to serve His purposes.

One of the worst things we can do for our worry is to lock God in a box that we invented. God has a million ways of providing for those who remain faithful to Him. It may not be a way that you expect, but if you will stay true to Him and His rule over your life, He will never let you be forsaken, or let your children beg for bread (Psalm 37:25).

Pursuing God's Presence in Prayer

> Yours, O LORD, is the greatness and the power and the glory and the victory and the majesty, indeed everything that is in the heavens and the earth; Yours is the dominion, O LORD, and You exalt Yourself as head over all. Both riches and honor come from You, and You rule over all, and in Your hand is power and might; and it lies in Your hand to make great and to strengthen everyone (1 Chronicles 29:11-12).

> You shall remember the LORD your God, for it is He who is giving you power to make wealth, that He may confirm His covenant which He swore to your fathers, as it is this day (Deuteronomy 8:18).

When you reap the harvest of your lan/
you shall not reap to the very corner/
nor gather the gleaning of your harvest; you
leave them for the needy and the alien. I am the
LORD your God (Leviticus 23:22).

Practice of Prayer

Gracious Lord, You own the cattle on a thousand hills. You are the maker and creator of all things. The stores of your kingdom never run out. Yours is the greatness and power and glory and victory—even everything that is in the heavens and the earth. Yours is the dominion, God, and You are exalted over all. Father, riches and honor come from You, and You are involved whether a nation is prosperous or the economy wanes.

Knowing this, my prayer is for Your mercy, God. Please shed Your mercy by the blood of Jesus Christ over our country and our economy. Too many in our nation have not honored You with the wealth of this land. In fact, we have used it to oppress others. So I beg for Your mercy over us all and over our country, because it is only by Your mercy that we will be blessed. We are not deserving of Your blessing, Lord, but Jesus Christ is our righteousness and it is by His name that I appeal before You.

Let my fears be put to rest as I turn my heart only to You. Limit my thoughts on what could happen and what may take place with regard to our national economy, and even with regard to my own finances. Let me think only of today and what today brings. Tomorrow has enough worries of its own. I look to You today, Lord, knowing that You are the sustainer of all things. I will find my peace in You, for You are able to give power to make wealth and to make a nation secure. In Christ's name, amen.

Personal Prayer Thoughts, Answers, and Reminders

_____

_____

_____

_____

_____

_____

_____

_____

_____

_____

_____

_____

_____

_____

_____

_____

_____

_____

_____

18

Family

Preparing Our Hearts for Prayer

Family is one of the greatest gifts God has given us to enjoy while on earth. The love and bond that takes place between the different familial relationships within marriage and the family carries a weight of love unlike any other. When an elderly person reaches their time to "go home" and pass into eternity, they never say they wished they would have spent more time on the job. The person always regrets not spending enough time with family. When life becomes rough and challenges arise, we are reminded just how important our families truly are.

That said, we can find ourselves worrying about numerous issues with regard to our families. We worry about the future of our children. Will they be safe? Will they walk with the Lord? Will they be healthy? Will they be blessed with a satisfying marriage and a home they enjoy? We worry whether or not we've done a good job fulfilling our role as a parent as well. Or as a spouse. A grandparent. Even as a child to our own parents.

Many of us have also reached a season in life when cares and concerns about our aging parents burden us. Where will they live? Are they secure where they are? How often can we go and visit them? Should they live with us? Juggling the demands of family responsibilities can take its toll on anyone. Imagining all the different ways that life could go wrong can be exhausting. Thus, when it comes to overcoming your worries and anxiety for matters concerning your family, as well as your worries about fulfilling your familial role, the antidote comes through casting these concerns onto the Lord. They are simply too much for you to bear alone.

Jesus tells us to come to Him. All who are weary and heavy laden will find our rest in Him. Yoking up with Him through obedience allows Him to carry the load for us. Obedience to Christ's instructions may not have been what you had expected to hear on how to overcome worry about family matters, but the closer you are to Christ, the more strength He supplies.

As you abide in Him, and His Word abides in you, you will be given all you need to release your anxious thoughts. A loving, intimate relationship with Jesus Christ provides you with the presence of peace amid the cares and concerns of this world. Nurture your walk with Him and your obedience to Him, and then watch Him lift you from the pit of worry into His delicate and protective care.

Pursuing God's Presence in Prayer

> If it is disagreeable in your sight to serve the LORD, choose for yourselves today whom you will serve: whether the gods which your fathers served which were beyond the River, or the gods of the Amorites in whose land you are living; but as for me and my house, we will serve the LORD (Joshua 24:15).

> May the LORD our God be with us, as He was with our fathers; may He not leave us or forsake us (1 Kings 8:57).

> These words, which I am commanding you today,

shall be on your heart. You shall teach them diligently to your sons and shall talk of them when you sit in your house and when you walk by the way and when you lie down and when you rise up (Deuteronomy 6:6-7).

Practice of Prayer

Heavenly Father, You are the ultimate overseer over my home and my loved ones. You are our caregiver, provider, and hope. May You always be with us as You have been with families throughout the Bible and throughout the ages. May You, Lord, neither leave us nor forsake us. Bind us together in Your love. Unite us under Your purpose and pleasure. In You, we are home.

Lord, give me wisdom on how to fulfill and live out the many roles I have in my family. Give me an ability to discern what needs to be done and how I can best contribute to the lives of my loved ones. Help me not to wallow in regret over things done wrong or not done in the past, but rather to embrace today and live out my role with kindness, compassion, grace, and patience.

Thank You, Lord, that You keep Your promise never to leave us or forsake us. Help me to let go of what I cannot control and to trust You with the well-being of my family members. In Christ's name, amen.

Personal Prayer Thoughts, Answers, and Reminders

_____

_____

_____

_____

_____

_____

_____

_____

_____

_____

_____

_____

_____

_____

_____

_____

_____

_____

_____

_____

_____

_____

_____

19

Travel

Preparing Our Hearts for Prayer

The fear of travel comes wrapped up in a multitude of fears. These include:

Fear of the unknown

Fear of leaving your comfort zone

Fear of harm in a foreign country

Fear of robbery

Fear of flying

Fear of trains

Fear of financial strain

You might have one or all of these fears wrapped up in your fear of travel, which can debilitate you to the point of never stepping out your front door. That fear is called *agoraphobia*, while the fear of traveling is called *hodophobia*. Regardless of the name, it can keep you homebound at worst and townbound at best. Symptoms of *hodophobia* when traveling include shaking, sweating, confusion, difficulty navigating routes or airports, headaches, gastrointestinal issues, and more.

So what is the antidote to overcoming this inner anxiety?

Getting a real sense of God's presence is one way to overcome your worry and anxiety with regard to travel. This is because when your spirit is finely tuned to His, you will experience the security of God being with you as you go. God will be with you when you travel because He is already here, there, and everywhere. If you are familiar with names of God in Scripture, you may have come across the name Jehovah Shammah. This unique name for God appears in the Bible only one time, in Ezekiel 48:35. The literal translation of the name means, "The LORD is there." While the context for this name of God has to do with the city of Jerusalem, the principle behind its meaning transcends into your travels. Wherever you may be going, the Lord is already there. Whatever trip you plan to take, the Lord is already there. Jehovah Shammah will not abandon you if you leave the comfort of your own home. In fact, many people report experiencing God in a fresh and personally meaningful way when they break free of their comfort zones and travel.

As you hide yourself in God, He surrounds you with His favor as a shield. If it helps, you can even imagine yourself in God's protective bubble that goes with you everywhere. That bubble is God's favor. Through it, He guards your going out and your coming in.

Overcoming worry and anxiety when it comes to traveling can be a challenge, and healing may not happen overnight. But there are other steps you can take in addition to drawing near to the Lord. For one, know what to expect. Visualize your trip by going online and looking at routes, milestones, familiar markers, and the general culture of your destination. See it before you get there so that when you arrive it won't feel so unnatural. Get plenty of sleep and be intentional about staying hydrated. Travel with a friend or family member. Familiarize yourself with traveling processes before you go. Print out a copy of all necessary paperwork, rather than solely relying on electronic means of planning. Pack for the unexpected so you won't be caught off guard in case of sickness or emergency. These tips can assist you with a smooth trip, but, as with any phobia, the greatest way for overcoming it is simply to expose yourself to it—slowly but surely, and repeatedly.

Pursuing God's Presence in Prayer

> Blessed shall you be when you come in, and blessed shall you be when you go out (Deuteronomy 28:6).

> For it is You who blesses the righteous man, O LORD, You surround him with favor as with a shield (Psalm 5:12).

> The LORD will guard your going out and your coming in from this time forth and forever (Psalm 121:8).

> Where can I go from Your Spirit? Or where can I flee from Your presence? If I ascend to heaven, You are there; if I make my bed in Sheol, behold, You are there. If I take the wings of the dawn, if I dwell in the remotest part of the sea, even there Your hand will lead me, and Your right hand will lay hold of me (Psalm 139:7-10).

Practice of Prayer

Dear Lord, You tell me that I am blessed when I come in and blessed when I go out. My blessing is not dependent on me staying in one location. Neither is my safety. Your name is Jehovah Shammah, meaning You are already there wherever I go. I may not know what to expect, Lord, but You do. I may not know what I will experience, but You do. When I rest in

You and put my trust in You, You prepare my steps before me so that all I need to do is walk in them. You are the great travel guide because this is Your world. You know the best places for me to travel and the best ways to get there. Grant me wisdom and courage to venture into this area of travel as I've never done before. Bless me with the ability, finances, and emotional strength to explore Your great creation boldly.

Cover me with traveling mercies, God. And relieve the fears that come upon me and the symptoms they produce. I put my trust and hope in You. You are the keeper of my soul and the protector of my life. Make my steps firm as I follow You in faith wherever You direct me to go. I love You, Lord, and thank You that I can talk to You openly about what makes me anxious—and You don't judge me. Instead, You are a quiet comfort and a measure of peace for my soul. In Christ's name, amen.

Personal Prayer Thoughts, Answers, and Reminders

_____

_____

_____

_____

_____

_____

_____

_____

_____

_____

_____

_____

_____

_____

_____

_____

_____

_____

_____

20

Spiritual Warfare

Preparing Our Hearts for Prayer

D o you have a coworker or family member who knows how to "push your buttons"? Or maybe you know how to push someone else's? It's a phrase we use to describe knowing where a weak point is in someone's life and how it causes them to respond poorly. Sometimes we push a button on purpose. Other times it's on accident. But every time, it's an annoyance and intrusion—something that gets under the skin. Right?

Well, people aren't the only ones who can do that. Satan is well-versed on your weak points. In fact, he knows where everyone's weak points are. For one person, it could be worrying about the health of a child. For another person, it might be flying on a plane. One person may fixate on finances, while another may worry about germs. Another person may experience debilitating anxiety over whether or not they will ever have meaningful relationships. Another person may fear going to a mall. For some it is a combination of all of the above, depending on the hour, day, or season of life.

Spiritual warfare is never a one-size-fits-all attack. Satan has been studying you for a very long time. He and his demons have been studying each of us, and when push comes to shove, he knows which buttons to push and when.

That's why being aware of spiritual warfare is step number one in overcoming it. When you think your spouse, a coworker, your boss, a neighbor, a TV news segment, a doctor, or a CPA is causing you the anxiety and stress you feel, you've got your eyes on the wrong culprit. Yes, people and situations have a part to play, but behind every physical activity we engage in on earth lies a spiritual trigger. God is an intentional God, and Satan is an intentional enemy.

A great antidote, then, to spiritual warfare involves asking God to open your eyes. Ask Him to let you see behind the scenes—just as in 2 Kings 6:17, when the prophet Elisha asked God to open his servant's eyes to see the angels and spiritual reality around them. We, too, can ask God to open our eyes. We may not see literal chariots of fire as the servant did, but we can see beyond the spiritual attack to find the root of the battle. The Bible says that every time we ask for wisdom, without doubting, God will give it (James 1:5).

As you face spiritual warfare in your life—and if you are a Christian, you will face it regularly—rather than succumbing to worry, ask for wisdom. God will give you wisdom on how to wage each battle before you.

Pursuing God's Presence in Prayer

> Put on the full armor of God, so that you will be able to stand firm against the schemes of the devil (Ephesians 6:11).

> Though we walk in the flesh, we do not war according to the flesh, for the weapons of our warfare are not of the flesh, but divinely powerful for the destruction of fortresses (2 Corinthians 10:3-4).

> He will give His angels charge concerning you, to guard you in all your ways (Psalm 91:11).

Practice of Prayer

King of Glory, Your Word says that You train my hands for war and my fingers for battle (Psalm 144:1). Teach my hands how to wage spiritual warfare, and instruct my fingers on how to fight. The weapons I am to use in spiritual warfare are not of the flesh. They are divinely powerful for the destruction of fortresses. Lord, give me the wisdom I need to use these weapons wisely. Also send out Your arrows and scatter the enemy. Remove those that are too strong for me. Deliver me and bring me into a spacious place full of peace.

I am Your child, and You give me deliverance. I pray to overcome any sifting that Satan seeks to do in my life. Cleanse my heart, Lord, so that I do not give Satan a stronghold from which to wage effective warfare against me. Lead me to repent of sins from which I have not yet turned, and strengthen my obedience to You. I resist the enemy and submit to God, trusting in His power and presence. I remain sober and aware, knowing that all authority has been given to Jesus and I am seated with Christ in the heavenlies. In Christ's name, amen.

Personal Prayer Thoughts, Answers, and Reminders

_____

_____

_____

_____

_____

_____

_____

_____

_____

_____

_____

_____

_____

_____

_____

_____

_____

_____

_____

Catalog of Scriptures to Overcome Worry

Be anxious for nothing, but in everything by prayer and supplication with thanksgiving let your requests be made known to God. And the peace of God, which surpasses all comprehension, will guard your hearts and your minds in Christ Jesus.

Philippians 4:6-7

I say to you, do not be worried about your life, as to what you will eat or what you will drink; nor for your body, as to what you will put on. Is not life more than food, and the body more than clothing? Look at the birds of the air, that they do not sow, nor reap nor gather into barns, and yet your heavenly Father feeds them. Are you not worth much more than they? And who of you by being worried can add a single hour to his life? And why are you worried about clothing? Observe how the lilies of the field grow; they do not toil nor do they spin, yet I say to you that not even Solomon in all his glory clothed himself like one of these. But if God so clothes the grass of the field, which is alive today and tomorrow is thrown into the furnace, will He not much more clothe you? You of little faith! Do not worry then, saying, "What will we eat?" or "What will we drink?" or "What will we wear for clothing?" For the Gentiles eagerly seek all these things; for your heavenly Father knows that you need all these things. But seek first His kingdom and His righteousness, and all these things will be added to you.

So do not worry about tomorrow; for tomorrow will care for itself. Each day has enough trouble of its own.

Matthew 6:25-34

Peace I leave with you; My peace I give to you; not as the world gives do I give to you. Do not let your heart be troubled, nor let it be fearful.

John 14:27

Trust in the LORD with all your heart and do not lean on your own understanding. In all your ways acknowledge Him, and He will make your paths straight.

Proverbs 3:5-6

My God will supply all your needs according to His riches in glory in Christ Jesus.

Philippians 4:19

What then shall we say to these things? If God is for us, who is against us?

Romans 8:31

Come to Me, all who are weary and heavy-laden, and I will give you rest. Take My yoke upon you and learn from Me, for I am gentle and humble in heart, and you will find rest for your souls. For My yoke is easy and My burden is light.

Matthew 11:28-30

Humble yourselves under the mighty hand of God, that He may exalt you at the proper time, casting all your anxiety on Him, because He cares for you.

1 Peter 5:6-7

Do not fear, for I am with you; do not anxiously look about you, for I am your God. I will strengthen you, surely I will help you, surely I will uphold you with My righteous right hand.

Isaiah 41:10

May the God of hope fill you with all joy and peace in believing, so that you will abound in hope by the power of the Holy Spirit.

Romans 15:13

There is no fear in love; but perfect love casts out fear, because fear involves punishment, and the one who fears is not perfected in love.

1 John 4:18

We know that God causes all things to work together for good to those who love God, to those who are called according to His purpose.

Romans 8:28

Faith is the assurance of things hoped for, the conviction of things not seen.

Hebrews 11:1

Do not fret because of evildoers, be not envious toward wrongdoers. For they will wither quickly like the grass and fade like the green herb. Trust in the LORD and do good; dwell in the land and cultivate faithfulness. Delight yourself in the LORD; and He will give you the desires of your heart.

Psalm 37:1-4

For you who fear My name, the sun of righteousness will rise with healing in its wings; and you will go forth and skip about like calves from the stall.

Malachi 4:2

I am the LORD your God, who upholds your right hand, who says to you, "Do not fear, I will help you."

Isaiah 41:13

The LORD is my shepherd; I shall not want. He makes me lie down in green pastures; He leads me beside quiet waters. He restores my soul; He guides me in the paths of righteousness for His name's sake. Even though I walk through the valley of the shadow of death, I fear no evil, for You are with me; Your rod and Your staff, they comfort me. You prepare a table before me in the presence of my enemies; You have anointed my head with oil; my cup overflows. Surely goodness and lovingkindness will follow me all the days of my life, and I will dwell in the house of the LORD forever.

Psalm 23:1-6

I urge you, brethren, by the mercies of God, to present your bodies a living and holy sacrifice, acceptable to God, which is your spiritual service of worship. And do not be conformed to this world, but be transformed by the renewing of your mind, so that you may prove what the will of God is, that which is good and acceptable and perfect.

Romans 12:1-2

God so loved the world, that He gave His only begotten Son, that whoever believes in Him shall not perish, but have eternal life.

John 3:16

Though the fig tree should not blossom and there be no fruit on the vines, though the yield of the olive should fail and the fields produce no food, though the flock should be cut off from the fold and there be no cattle in the stalls, yet

I will exult in the LORD, I will rejoice in the God of my salvation. The Lord GOD is my strength, and He has made my feet like hinds' feet, and makes me walk on my high places.

Habakkuk 3:17-19

Cease striving and know that I am God; I will be exalted among the nations, I will be exalted in the earth.

Psalm 46:10

The LORD also will be a stronghold for the oppressed, a stronghold in times of trouble; and those who know Your name will put their trust in You, for You, O LORD, have not forsaken those who seek You.

Psalm 9:9-10

Everyone who thirsts, come to the waters; and you who have no money come, buy and eat. Come, buy wine and milk without money and without cost. Why do you spend money for what is not bread, and your wages for what does not satisfy? Listen carefully to Me, and eat what is good, and delight yourself in abundance. Incline your ear and come to Me. Listen, that you may live; and I will make an everlasting covenant with you, according to the faithful mercies shown to David.

Isaiah 55:1-3

Do not let your heart be troubled; believe in God, believe also in Me.

John 14:1

The Lord is faithful, and He will strengthen and protect you from the evil one.

2 Thessalonians 3:3

Jesus said to her, "Did I not say to you that if you believe, you will see the glory of God?"

John 11:40

The LORD is my light and my salvation; whom shall I fear? The LORD is the defense of my life; whom shall I dread?

Psalm 27:1

A battered reed He will not break off, and a smoldering wick He will not put out, until He leads justice to victory.

Matthew 12:20

See how great a love the Father has bestowed on us, that we would be called children of God; and such we are. For this reason the world does not know us, because it did not know Him.

1 John 3:1

Bless the LORD, O my soul, and all that is within me, bless His holy name. Bless the LORD, O my soul, and forget none of His benefits; who pardons all your iniquities, who heals all your diseases; who redeems your life from the pit, who crowns you with lovingkindness and compassion;

who satisfies your years with good things, so that your youth is renewed like the eagle.

Psalm 103:1-5

Many are the sorrows of the wicked, but he who trusts in the LORD, lovingkindness shall surround him.

Psalm 32:10

Cast your burden upon the LORD and He will sustain you; He will never allow the righteous to be shaken.

Psalm 55:22

We confidently say, "The Lord is my helper, I will not be afraid. What will man do to me?"

Hebrews 13:6

Consider it all joy, my brethren, when you encounter various trials, knowing that the testing of your faith produces endurance. And let endurance have its perfect result, so that you may be perfect and complete, lacking in nothing.

James 1:2-4

These things I have spoken to you, so that in Me you may have peace. In the world you have tribulation, but take courage; I have overcome the world.

John 16:33

By this the love of God was manifested in us, that God has sent His only begotten Son into the world so that we might live through Him. In this is love, not that we loved God, but that He loved us and sent His Son to be the propitiation for our sins.

1 John 4:9-10

Anxiety in a man's heart weighs it down, but a good word makes it glad.

Proverbs 12:25

I have been young and now I am old, yet I have not seen the righteous forsaken or his descendants begging bread.

Psalm 37:25

Notes

1. Christopher Bergland, "How Does Medicine Reduce Anxiety at a Neural Level?" *Psychology Today*, June 7, 2013, https://www.psychologytoday.com/blog/the-athletes-way/201306/how-does-meditation-reduce-anxiety-neural-level.

2. Carolyn Gregoire, "What Constant Exposure to Negative News Is Doing to Our Mental Health," *Huffington Post*, February 9, 2015, http://www.huffingtonpost.com/2015/02/19/violent-media-anxiety_n_6671732.html.

3. Charles C.W. Cooke, "Careful with the Panic: Violent Crime and Gun Crime Are Both Dropping," *National Review*, November 30, 2015, http://www.nationalreview.com/corner/427758/careful-panic-violent-crime-and-gun-crime-are-both-dropping-charles-c-w-cooke. Accessed February 6, 2017.

4. Alexandra Sifferlin, "Divorce More Likely When Wife Falls Ill," *Time*, May 1, 2014, http://time.com/83486/divorece-is-more-likely-if-the-wife-not-the-husband-gets-sick/.

5. Scott Clement and Julie Eilperin, "Americans More Fearful of a Major Terrorist Attack in the U.S., Poll Finds," *Washington Post*, November 20, 2015, https://www.washingtonpost.com/politics/americans-more-fearful-of-a-major-terror-attack-in-the-us-poll-finds/2015/11/20/ec6310ca-8f9a-11e5-ae1f-af46b7df8483_story.html. Accessed March 29, 2017.

6. Dhruv Khullar, "How Social Isolation Is Killing Us," *The New York Times*, December 22, 2016, http://www.nytimes.com/2016/12/22/upshot/how-social-isolation-is-killing-us.html.

7. Guy Winch, PhD, "Loneliness Increases Chances of Early Death by 14%," *Psychology Today*, February 19, 2014, https://www.psychologytoday.com/blog/the-squeaky-wheel/201402/loneliness-increases-chances-early-death-14.

8. Kathryn Dill, "Survey: 42% of Employees Have Changed Jobs Due to Stress," *Forbes*, April 18, 2014, https://www.forbes.com/sites/kathryndill/2014/04/18/survey-42-of-employees-have-changed-jobs-due-to-stress/#611ed31e3380. Accessed March 29, 2017.

WANT A TASTE OF WHAT IT MEANS TO DREAM AGAIN?

Join Bruce Wilkinson for this life-changing 12-week course and learn the strategies to re-engage with your passions and truly live your dream.

Unlock your dream through exclusive access to this online, self-paced course offering:

· Brand NEW weekly video lessons from Bruce
· Course content
· Personal study & reflection
· A pathway to pursue your dreams!

Discover the future you've only dreamed of before!

DREAM AGAIN

12-WEEK COURSE

BRUCE WILKINSON

BruceWilkinson.com

To learn more about Harvest House books and
to read sample chapters, visit our website:

www.harvesthousepublishers.com

HARVEST HOUSE PUBLISHERS
EUGENE, OREGON